ALSO BY DIANE WAKOSKI

Coins & Coffins (1962)
Four Young Lady Poets (1962)
Discrepancies and Apparitions (1966)
The George Washington Poems (1967)
Greed: Parts 1 & 2 (1968)
The Diamond Merchant (1968)
Inside the Blood Factory (1968)
Thanking My Mother for Piano Lessons (1969)
The Lament of the Lady Bank Dick (1969)
Greed: Parts 3 & 4 (1969)
The Moon Has a Complicated Geography (1969)
Black Dream Ditty (1970)
The Magellanic Clouds (1970)
Greed: Parts 5-7 (1971)
On Barbara's Shore (1971)
The Motorcycle Betrayal Poems (1971)
Form Is an Extension of Content (1972)
Smudging (1972)
The Pumpkin Pie (1972)
Greed: Parts 8, 9 & 11 (1973)
Dancing on the Grave of a Son of a Bitch (1973)
Looking for the King of Spain (1974)
Trilogy: Coins & Coffins, Discrepancies and
    Apparitions, The George Washington Poems (1974)
The Fable of the Lion and the Unicorn (1975)
Creating a Personal Mythology (1975)
The Wandering Tattler (1975)
Virtuoso Literature for Two and Four Hands (1975)
Variations on a Theme (1976)
Waiting for the King of Spain (1976)
Pachelbel's Canon (1978)
The Man Who Shook Hands (1978)
Trophies (1979)
Cap of Darkness (1980)
The Magician's Feastletters (1982)

DIANE WAKOSKI

THE COLLECTED GREED PARTS 1-13

**BLACK SPARROW PRESS
SANTA BARBARA ··· 1984**

THE COLLECTED GREED, PARTS 1-13. Copyright © 1968, 1969, 1971, 1973, 1984 by Diane Wakoski.

All rights reserved. Printed in the United States of America. No part of this book may be used or reproduced in any manner whatsoever without written permission except in the case of brief quotations embodied in critical articles and reviews. For information address Black Sparrow Press, P.O. Box 3993, Santa Barbara, CA 93130.

LIBRARY OF CONGRESS CATALOGING IN PUBLICATION DATA

Wakoski, Diane.
  The collected greed, parts 1-13.

  I. Title.
PS3573.A42G69   1984   811'.54   84-12416
ISBN 0-87685-463-3
ISBN 0-87685-464-1 (signed ed.)
ISBN 0-87685-462-5 (pbk.)

for Robert

Preface

Sometime in 1967 I had a letter from John Martin. I was living in New York City. He was in Los Angeles, and introduced himself as someone serious about contemporary poetry who was starting a press and interested in publishing something of mine. I think Robert Kelly had told him about me. He said that if I had any work at hand that I thought might be too experimental for other publishers or was working on something interesting that he would like to see it.

Talk about timing. I had been thinking for the past year or so about my poetry getting locked into itself, worried that having found an identifiable voice, I might start imitating it. Diminishing it. I believe the manuscript for *Inside the Blood Factory* was already at Doubleday, and I felt a bigness about that book, and a completeness which froze me. I was being exposed to the New York school of poets through my connection with St. Mark's Poetry Project and beginning to wonder how I could utilize the kind of sensitivity to "trivia"—the everyday sense of things—in my own poems that Frank O'Hara and others had voiced in theirs. I also was being assaulted by violent feelings about what was happening in the domestic life of Robert Kelly, worried and terrified by the schism between him and his first wife, Joby, and the polygamous situation I thought was developing.

John's letter was like a royal permission for me to do something taboo. I decided I wanted to write a long, preachy, didactic poem, using personal and trivial details, names of people, and even gossipy hearsay. I wanted to pontificate about life, to moralize, and yet somehow to write a poem which would have a nobility to it. I decided that I would write this long poem in four parts, call it *GREED,* and hope that it wouldn't be too controversial or difficult for John to want to publish.

Because I was still afraid of what I really wanted to do, I did set some rules for myself in composing the poem. I decided that each of the four sections or parts of the poem would have a presiding metaphor in the form of a cold-blooded animal or creature that symbolized the kind of greed on which I was going to focus in that part. I felt this would give the poem a larger scope and carry it somewhat beyond the realm of the newspaperish sort of things which the New York school poets were writing. I chose polygamy as the subject for the first part and decided, with my classic fear of snakes, to use the copperhead snake as my presiding metaphor.

The second part, "Of Accord and Principle," came out of the daily grit of poetry politics and trying to earn a living as a young poet. I have always been apolitical in my poetry, and I hated the whole Vietnam period because this war invaded the poems and poetry readings. I never wrote anti-war poems or indulged in what I perceived as fashion-mongering by some political poets of the late sixties and early seventies. I tried to cling to my own personal politics of absolute honesty and was amazed and outraged when a school librarian censured me, after a Poets in the Schools reading, saying that I should be barred because of "that word" I had used. Compared to most poetry of that era which was studded with "fucks," "shits," and other violent language, along with wildly stated political ideas, my poetry seemed rather demure and even prissy. But I did have a poem about a painful family situation with an autistic child, an alcoholic father, etc., called "Slicing Oranges for Jeremiah," which I had read. It refers to the child not having control over his bowels and contains the word "shit" instead of "excrement" or some other less vivid equivalent. It took me an hour to realize what the librarian must have meant when she referred to "that word" in my poem. At any rate, I decided never to participate in Poets in the Schools again, as I was also pissed-off at the kind of wheeling and dealing which went on in the context of these political jobs. This was coupled with my annoyance with anti-war readings and highly publicized events like the reading of the Russian poet Voznesensky.

These two poems were sent to John Martin who accepted them at once, and they were published as *GREED, Parts 1 & 2* in 1968. My first Black Sparrow book. It goes without saying that *GREED* expanded and became more than the four parts I had originally intended. And I do not know if there are still more parts to follow "Part 13," which ends this book, or whether "Part 10" will ever be written. Once I had gone beyond "Part 4," I wanted an open-end poem that I could spend the rest of my life writing if I wanted to. And I still think, in that sense, that *GREED* remains open-ended, even though with the completion of "Part 13" I am quite ready for a *COLLECTED GREED*.

When I wrote the first two parts of *GREED* I felt that I had produced something quite different from the rest of my work. But over the years I have found that no one else sees the differences. Perhaps by giving me permission to break my own rules and write a drastically different new work, John Martin didn't generate a new side of Wakoski, but simply allowed me the possibility of growing and expanding, for getting from one place to another. I do know that whatever the case proves to be, I will always be in John's debt for suggesting the possibility of such a poem. I continue to be in his debt for bearing with me and with this poem, even now, in its newest and most uncomfortable parts.

Diane Wakoski
East Lansing, Michigan
August 11, 1983

Table of Contents

Preface		7
GREED, Part 1:	*Of Polygamy*	15
GREED, Part 2:	*Of Accord & Principle*	23
GREED, Part 3:	*The Greed That Is Not Greed*	35
GREED, Part 4:	*Intruders*	45
GREED, Part 5:	*The Shark — Parents & Children*	57
GREED, Part 6:	*Jealousy — A Confessional*	71
GREED, Part 7:	*Self-Righteousness*	83
GREED, Part 8:	*The Desire To Be What One Is Not While Clinging To What One Is*	95
GREED, Part 9:	*The Water Element Song For Sylvia*	105
GREED, Part 10:	*A Note*	121
GREED, Part 11:	*Power*	125
GREED, Part 12:	*The Greed To Be Fulfilled*	143
GREED, Part 13:	*The Greed For Control Over Death & Life*	227

THE COLLECTED GREED

Parts 1–13

GREED, Part 1

Of Polygamy

This is
an invitation
for you to touch
me, my body
the tiger lily
growing in the powdered coffee dirt

        the copperhead
        winds around a man's limbs
        when he is little;
        he says he remembers it
        tightening against his leg
        as a rubber band.

A set of veins and arteries
keeps our blood going
in the right directions;
a circular movement
where opposites are part of the same flow
but now you
cut off my circulation
and expect me to
digest the poison setting into
my system,

no poison I say,
but the blood backed up
and now looking for other circuits
to flow;
the body, not a reservoir,
the mind not a dam.

        How did the snake unwind from his leg,
            I asked him.
        It bit and spiraled off the leg,
        disappearing

as a trickle of blood
into the grass,
his body not growing like an orange flower
in the rich dirt,
rather,
cutting off the flow
of energy,
the sex backing up
damming his body;
this was an invitation
to cut off
his body.

Not until later did he find two women
who needed him, one for the mind,
one for the body,
not able to choose the two sources having
been
diverted,
the choice not being possible,

an old prison,
the copperhead wound around his leg
rupturing the veins.

I never encountered
this problem,
my life having
been full of deprivations.
Choice was a watch never presented to me at graduation.

Loss was a light turned on at night,
something I was used to
and used to
read and write by;

a young husband with curls flowing out of his head
like peas from the barrel,

a man riding with rings on his fingers,
bells in his ears,
presenting all the love,
enough to tumble around me as books would if
you were to tip over all the shelves at the library;
a richness,

again no choice but this time
a bounty,
beauty flooding my life,
no compunctions about the high price,

but then the ocean came
between us,
4,000 miles of Atlantic salt
and the bounty was not over,
the rains
perhaps of tears
had been heavy this year
swollen the lands with food, meat plenty,
biscuits crumblingly white under the butter;

forgive me, my greed never before present,
never provoked, arrived
like a cloud of mosquitoes on a muggy day.

I was/am presented with more beautiful men
who would ride their black motorcycles to death for me
or photograph my braincells with eight eyes
making all the colors of my hair
reflect in the moon,
make tiger lilies grow on my surrealist pillow,
and only the thin cable
resisting the waves of the Atlantic,
the erosion of strong salt
connected us, my husband,
and I,
a voice the fish would not interpret,

No, I said,
to all his demands,
my heart parachuting from every plane he asked me to take

> he would put the salt in my food again
> all the salt in the Atlantic
> I would grow thin and pale and the moon
> would shock my mouth with its size again
> then he would go away again
> I said
> or dam up my circuits again
>
> Greed wrapped its copperhead around my leg
> trying to make me
> unwrap the cellophane from my heart,
> rattle the paper noisily
> and break the candy in parts,
> hand it around to all the little boys,
> fly to London and be my husband's wife,
> his curls tumbling over me
> as sand in a broken hourglass
> until I choked
> my ears filled with it.

Greed blending in with the grass,
as I walk barefooted
holding the large hand of a man in the rain,
this time many hands reaching out to touch me,
distracting me from careful walking
the copperhead lurking there to wind around my leg
as it did around the leg of the greedy man
when he was a child,
the man with two wives
and too much of everything.

It was cold in March
and April; cold enough to keep me coiled
tightly under the mulch.

My eyes,
two tiger lilies,
burned and tried to keep me alive,
watching you
as you said you wanted to be a bachelor;
and I suppose
even the most beautiful snake
rippling its copperhead patterns under the
soft covering of leaves
could not be a temptation to love
to put your arms around; was that I,
shivering in March, in April,
with you,
refusing to give me the sun, stealing
it out of my plate each night
as I arose to eat it.

And now the sun has slipped into me
exploding my body, as the ripples of a rock
thrown into a pool, or a volcano erupting under the ocean.

Greed inches out of my mouth.
It is an invitation
for you
to touch
me, my body,

the tiger lilies have opened so wide
scattering their orange and freckled lips
around my ankles.
March and April I remember,
March and April shivering.

The greedy copperhead
wraps around my body,
strangling me
with the fear that I
will never get warm

enough.
Now I cannot ignore
the man with two wives
his problem,
or dismiss it,
oh bad child of nature that I am,
not knowing how to handle a local snake
the common copperhead
which wraps around my leg
and I
not a needy child any longer.

GREED, Part 2

Of Accord & Principle

The whole story
comes in
many segments, I see,
from each mouth that tells it
to me,
        as those tube-lipped goldfish
        swimming mouth to mouth
        in their aquarium,
        the kissing fish,
        we called them;
        we, trying to decide what nourishment
        they were deriving
        nibbling at each other's pale gold lips
        what words passed through the tissue and move
          the water
        exactly
        as your breath would stir my hair.
What happened?
We have as hard a time telling
as if there were no words.
Each voice tells articulately
its own story.
Nowhere
do they come together;
the kissing lips of the fish
who, we plainly see,
do not know what
kissing is.
        Was there one person who said a word
        that was
        forbidden?
        It started last year with "fuck the president,"
        words of political protest, quoted
        from a newspaper article
        and
        then there were reports of

others,
who said words that were
forbidden

and there were those of us who were
talking to the young as if they
could understand, and as if they were older than they
  were
and perhaps that is all that happened;
that what was
forbidden,
was to speak inappropriately to
children.

It all sounded
like the kissing fish,
the palest lips,
those who could say the least,
who did not know what kissing was about,
perhaps were giving the impression
as do those golden pale creatures, swimming in the
aquarium, that they were doing something, knowing,
loving,
a gesture of communication and
recognition
but then no one knew,
and it turned out that maybe we had all done something
forbidden.

The whole story is about poets who
read
or said
words
that were forbidden.
They said, "fuck the president,"
and in other cases
untraceable things.
They said what they had to say,

each one,
about the world
and they were saying it for money;
there was money to spread over the poets,
as fish food sprinkled
too abundantly
by an amateur
on the skin of the water
or
in some cases
the scum that forms
when there is no water animal
such as the snail
to keep the water clean;
but with the money came rules,
and certain words were forbidden
and in many cases no one knew what was said that was
forbidden;
an old Italian lady complained.
She couldn't say what had been said
but it offended. She said,
"you or I might speak one way when we are home and in private
but we don't speak that way before children;
we might be vulgar or gross
but we keep our poetry beautiful,
we don't walk on the grass,
we keep it beautiful";
and no one knew
no one could find out
but something was forbidden it was said
and it should not have been said.

It was greed on the part of the poets.
Wanting both accord and principle.
Wanting the felicity of $100 and still wanting to say what they
    thought,
as if the world, or any government would pay
a man $100 for his integrity;

25

27

maybe, if he pleases, and he polishes,
he kisses enough pale gold mouths
in deep meaningless kisses
as those fish who swim so, lips touching,
not knowing anything about commitment or love,
the government of city or state
will pay someone $100
to say something
beautiful
and safe.

The greed is of a poet who wants to be paid for his words
even if they are forbidden.
That is no different from the policeman who takes a bribe and still
wants to be considered doing his job.
That is no different a greed from that of a man who wants two
   wives
or a woman who wants to eat cake twice a day and still be thin.

I cannot chronicle all the greed of
accord and principle,
but can tell you that in this case
there was
       the greed of a woman who wanted everyone to like her;
       who wanted to make rules and still have the anarchists
          love her;
       who wanted to pay the poets for quality and integrity
       and then have them give it up, if it just meant changing
          a word or two;
       who wanted to make choices — saying this man is suitable,
       this one is not, and
       still have the man who was deemed not suitable
       to think her fair and equitable;
       who wanted to keep secrets and not be thought deceitful;
there was
       the greed of a young man who wanted to sleep with all
          the women available;
       who wanted to make his poems please everyone and at

the same time, to be thought unique, forceful,
a speaker of important words;
who wanted to make the extra money other poets were
losing when they were controversial;
who wanted the attention from knowing the secrets
that were kept by others,
and telling those secrets;
there was
the greed of a poet who wanted to be included in
everything;
there was
my greed,
after my spirit had been broken many times,
wanting money to make me believe my life, my poems
had some meaning;
there was
the greed of all poets,
wanting the luxury of a life dedicated to writing words,
as many as there are drops of water in a lake,
expressing himself and being paid for this self-indulgence.
There can be no greater joy than making a poem or a story or a picture that tells about you, your thoughts, your life, your feelings. In this case Emerson was right. If there is any virtue in being an artist, that virtue is its own reward. Why then, expect the world to applaud you, to honor you, to pay you for your pleasure, your indulgence? But that is the greed of all of us, the poets, who want our play considered work; want to be respected and paid for saying what we think and feel. Such luxury.

The fish with the cupped and pale gold lips
swimming in the tank
gesture meaninglessly,
kissing constantly.
Poets appear
endorsing the validity of each other's feelings.
They decide
who

really
feels
and
who's
a fake. They
decide that one expresses his feelings
too easily,
or another
without enough ease,
but when there are lips of rich fat poet fish to kiss
or the lips of editor fish
or national book award fish
or whisper fish, who have the ears of editors, publishers, and
organizers of reading tours,
their lips grow paler and paler gold
from kissing so much and so frequently
in the ferny aquarium.

But the one kiss they save
above all kisses
is for what they call
"integrity." They are all kissing and telling
who has
and who doesn't have
integrity. And the ones who kiss the most,
talk the most about
integrity.
There is no one of us
who hasn't done this;
who isn't at some time or other
swimming in the aquarium
with all the kissing poet fish
forgetting how the artificial light
makes the gold of our
scaled bodies
glimmer;
the lips, our lips
touch

30

as if they are rings of neon fire;
forgetting our own greed
with indignant talk of others' integrity. There is no way
to be honest
and to be paid for it. There is no
way to keep your soul and sell it too.

           Even Charles Olson
whose lesson to us has been
"don't let anything be easy;
make it hard"
speaking in Berkeley said that he sat
suffering
suffering in Gloucester
while others gained power,
and he craved power,
while he sat suffering in a town that smelled fishy,
but he craved love more,
and all the time he loved, he gave up power.
The acknowledgment
that we all crave too much,
want too much
is important.
What is hard
is to make the choice
to choose one over the other,
when both are so tempting,
so hard and smooth and easy to touch.

Greed is the taste of meat after many many weeks of fish.

And my own greed is always there,
like the jungle-movie image of piranhas waiting in the river
for one open wound,
even a cut, glistening a little, on the finger,
waiting for the offered blood to trigger the appetites
and allow those small mouths to tear all the flesh
from the bone.

Greed for everything,
    for respect
    for love
    for ease, peace,
days full of stories that would roll on my tongue
like mythical silver pears,
nights that would be a greenhouse
rich black earth covered with moss,
every flower, a calix to drink from,
breathe into,
loving me,
loving me more than anyone ever could

greed —
wanting the rewards that come from hard work
while still trying to have ease;
wanting the wisdom that comes from a hard and suffering life
while still trying not to be hurt;
the greedy man
is the one who will not choose.
My greed comes through even here,
forgive me,
I see things,
how they are,
I want to tell you about them,
I want, as Clayton said, to show the shit I've seen
in that pure world of poetry,
on the clean, well-manicured hands, jeweled with hypocrisy
    this is the pearl that was a lie
        this is the emerald that was a lie
        this is the ruby
        the sapphire
        they were all lies
I want to scream about it,
but I can't even say names,
I want to say names and not suffer the consequences
for my honesty
my truth.

I am no better, no different.
Let me tell you,
we are all torn in this world
apart by our desires,
our greed.

I will never forget going to a birthday party some twenty years ago when I was a child. We were the poorest family in my school, except for the Mexican fruit pickers' children, but brains are aristocracy in early age. I went to the party, not seeing carpets, polished wood, as many books as the public library had, private bedrooms, shiningly plumbed bathrooms (more than one), not seeing these things for the first time, but realizing, realizing for the first time, how different it was from our two-room house with the broken sagging screened porch, from my life. What gave me the strongest shock was the silverware, laid out on the lace table cloth. It was the most beautiful thing I had ever seen, long thick silver forks gleaming with heavy patterns; knife blades so smooth I thought they were liquid; spoons that felt heavy and cold in my hand. That silverware is all I remember of the party; it was a beauty I had never had in my life. It was a beauty. It was a beauty I wanted, not to own, but to be near.

My greed,
my greatest greed,
is that I have tried to create that opulence around me,
amass my fortune,
greedily,
but in words—not in possessions—
words which no one could spend,
which could never be used up,
which could never be taken away from me,
which could never be used as accusations against me
(as the rich and comfortable are always denounced).

I come
asking your admiration for my modesty,
while keeping this hoard under my tongue,
under the lid of my eye when I daydream,
under my fingers when I write at an empty table
in a bare room.

Admire me for my frugality, I say,
or my life full of bones and deserts,
but my words too
are as meaningless as the kissing fish;
behind my plainface
are the most lush and sybaritic dreams.

Look at
the kissing fish
swimming through the china bridges
around the toothy coral reef,
pale golden lips
touching
in a mockery of love—
touching
without feeling or meaning.

<u>Greed is an unwillingness to give up one thing
for another.</u>
You cannot have harmony, accord, agreement,
and also your integrity;
a maintenance of principle.

One kiss too many
and kisses lose their meanings.
Look at your own pale lips
reflected in the water.
Paler gold
and paler gold
from the greed; never stopping
not relinquishing one kiss.

GREED, Part 3

The Greed That Is Not Greed

(a poem with no universals, with very personal histories
& exploring a subject mentioned by Robert Kelly)

RARELY do I let myself
   write, mentioning real names or places.
   But in discussing the matter of greed,
   I, always slightly overweight according to *Vogue*
    standards
and living in the richest country in the world,
would not be fairly using the material at hand
were I not to speak of my experiences.
Robert Kelly is overweight.
I do not believe that it is greed that makes him eat
too much,
but hunger.
He probably does not eat much more than George
   Washington
who was about the same height (6′ 4″),
but his body makes fat out of the food.
In my original concept of greed,
I judged anything in excess to be a result of greed.
Kelly pointed out that this is not strictly
true.
Greed is motivated by deprivation & resultant
   pettiness.
Many things done in excess by one man's standard
are only the norm
by another's.
If I were to require a 350 pound man to eat my daily
   diet,
I would starve him.
And once you accept this,
you accept the concept of the variable norm.
The Variable Norm.
Once it is variable
who is to say it is a standard any longer?

Over a period of years
    having been a somewhat social person
    I have definitely seen many acts of greed.
    An act out of a desire of excess
    that leads to a man's debasement
    is greed.
    Having 2 wives
    if it divides your house
    your mind
    or your loyalties
    is an act of greed. But generosity
    would not necessarily
    have a better result. The greed, perhaps,
    is not in having 2 women
    but in having 2 who cannot live in the same house with peace
    or 2 whom you do not love equally, thus giving hurt to one,
    or 2 because of habit or convenience,
    not because 1 will not be enough,
    or 2 because you cannot tell one to go away.

But supply and demand are vicious forces,
    making a man wallow when there is plenty
    and cry when there's not enough.
    The ungreedy eats the same every day,
    saving the plenty to augment the sparse.
    In any area where you've conquered supply and demand
    you've conquered greed.
    For instance, Diane, the wife of the Hawk's Well Head,
    who told me she'd never pay $30 for a dress
    because whether she were rich or poor, it seemed like
    the wrong price.
    Some of the richest men
    walk around from year to year
    with a fixed idea of how much something should cost.
    And with that stability
    they are seldom at the mercy
    of their fortunes.
    In matters of money

    at least
    they have no greed.

Every time I think of greed,
    I think of the bitterness it causes,
    of what it takes away from others,
    how it destroys some balance
    that we are all trying to set up.
    Putting one thing above all others
    usually results in some form of greed.
    It is true that we usually look at our one obsession in life
    as a right, because we are willing to
    sacrifice other parts of our life for it;
    but there is no such thing as self-sacrifice
    without hurting others.
    Only a complete hermit and orphan can say
    that by following his greedy obsession to be alone
    he is hurting or depriving no one.
    We are social creatures;
    all our actions reflect back to others.

Rarely do I express my hostilities
    without also defending the person
    I feel anger towards.
    Sometimes defending him more than
    he would himself.
    I feel that to express anger
    without also giving mitigating circumstances
    or explanations
    is a greed. And that greed destroys
    the greedy.
    My anger with Carol Bergé
    that beautiful black orchid of the Chelsea
    for her poison pen letter to me
    in December 1967 telling me that I am too aggressive
      (Blaming it,
    of course, on some poor constellation in the sky which
      happened

to harbor the sun when I was born)
has made me so angry
that I constantly find it necessary to say nice things
    about her
even when no one else wants to.

It is a choice of greeds, sometimes.
When I would rather like everyone than hate anyone.
But there is a greed which is not greed. It is the
    desire to have,
to know, to experience, be,
everything,
so that you can share it, possess it with the world.
Desire
for the purpose of control or
excluding others
or of total ownership
is greed
whether motivated out of extreme need
or sheer petulance.
The effect can only debase the spirit.
Clayton Eshleman is often accused of being greedy
    for power.
He edits a literary magazine;
he has deep political commitments;
he left his wife in a very unsympathetic manner
because of a desire to shape his life differently
    than he could living
in her presence.
He, like Kelly, is not greedy for power.
He suffers from the greed which is not greed.
The greed to know everything,
to be everything,
to say everything.
But it is a desire to be complete with the world
and there accompanies it
a willingness to share all,
to include all,

      to give all.
           Provided he / they are given all.
That demand
          to be given all
yes, it is a greed.
But a greed that in the long run
is not
greed;
perhaps if sustained long enough,
carried far enough
becomes
greatness.

Telling Ted Berrigan,
    as a point of honor or integrity
    (and beware of the users of that last word,
    the breeding of self-righteousness)
    that I don't like his poems,
    is an act of greed on my part.
    His life is as honest as anyone's.
    His poems are as important to him
    as mine are to me.
    He has a different style
    a different way of life
    a different set of values
    but whereas I don't like his poems any less
    than I like the poems of lots of other poets,
    I don't like the way he treats his wife,
    and so I put him down publicly.
    <u>It is a sign of rotten moral greed</u>
    <u>to be so frugal with approval.</u>
    The greed of a man who can genuinely like everyone,
    maybe just because they're human beings,
    is the greed that is not greed.
    Do not confuse this with wanting everyone to like you.

Kelly has a talent of giving
    that, even with the best of intentions,

few others could show.
Perhaps it is that he has the language
to communicate to everyone.
Most of my friends are good people
as well as good poets
in my judgment.
None of them are greed-less
but most are intelligent
and know what their greed is
and how to compensate for it.
Jerome Rothenberg is greedy for peace & harmony
having lived all the centuries of the Jew's persecution
in his mind.
David Antin is greedy for authority on every subject.
Jackson Mac Low is greedy to write every poem
    at least once, try
every idea.
Armand Schwerner to unite science and art.
Rochelle Owens to say every swear word and have
    every erotic
experience.
Jack Anderson to make everything unusual.
Paul Blackburn to be able to talk to anyone, on any level, &
communicate.

<u>Everyone has his own greed</u>
    <u>and suffers from it. It stops being greed</u>
    <u>when it is understood</u>
    <u>and compensated for.</u> When it leads to
a greater product
a fullness
otherwise not there.
The greed that is not greed
benefits others,
even while destroying some part of you. *ego?*

Lonely poets. We need to be alone to think.
    Our hallucinations creep up on us

and scare us into company. We talk.
We tell everything we dreamed or felt,
what we saw in the dark,
the stone breathing,
the trees pulling our hair.

Lying poets. Making up stories
    to exonerate ourselves,
    to hide the greed.
    <u>It is not necessary</u>.

Young children don't hide their needs.
    They don't hide desire either.
    The greed that is not greed
    goes one step beyond the scratch in the phonograph
        record,
    the spot that repeats over & over,
    cannot get beyond itself.
    The man who acknowledges his ill
    that he needs more than the norm or more than others
        allow
    and who takes it, in the face of all accusations,
    but gives it back with interest.
    <u>He is the great man. The man who</u>
    <u>takes greed beyond greed.</u>

GREED, Part 4

Intruders

This child is born
just having sloughed off his tail
into some blood stream
after nine months of tasting salt
and feeling warm water
touch his cheeks;
sometimes he drops feet first into the world
ready to run,
but usually head first
battering a path with his skull.

How many of us are born
as intruders,
unwanted nuisances,
ugly noisy holes
to be plugged?

Anyone who has entered as an intruder,
whose small unshod feet
walked only on floors that belonged to others,
whose hands tried to touch objects
which always belonged to others and were snatched away,
whose very words or cries were impositions
on someone else's place or time;
anyone of us who spent his first years
as an intruder
will spend his life trying to overcome
the feeling
that nothing belonged to him;
we were welcome no place,
there was nothing we could do that was not grudgingly tolerated;
we took up space that was not ours,
time that did not belong to us,
energy that could have been used more happily elsewhere,
money that could have been spent on something else,
food that no one wanted to give us,

even the affection or love that came,
perhaps just for our small helplessness,
was intended for someone else
and spilled accidentally
like a bottle of ink
under a dragging sleeve,
on us.

The intruders,
we,
who had nothing to give,
whose existence was interpreted as a burden,
pennies that would not go in a nickel slot,
oil on water.

Is it any wonder that we wind ourselves in thick shells
(like turtles)
of possessions,
deeds,
documents of ownership,
titles to right of way,
licenses giving us legal rights,
diplomas,
credentials?
We try to secure ourselves against loss
of love,
of houses,
of food,
of jobs,
of honor,
of dignity,
of identity.
We become landlords of the emotions.

BEING A LANDLORD OF THE EMOTIONS

Breaking off inside me
is a thin narrow bone of contention
          / called a poet /
a star or Baltimore oriole
gummed-sticker from a good piano lesson,
a cactus rose
whose succulent flat face,
as a lettuce,
or Mexican girl
in embroidered white blouse
bares its small teeth
in a smile.

This accident,
this river
of feelings,
making me need a spool of gold jeweler's wire
to tie down my fluttering heart,
the one that teeters
uneasily in high heels,
a heart making its first appearance.

What happened?
How was I born to worry so much
about the possibilities
of loneliness?

I think I am a man who worships
his own prisons;
why else would I be so concerned about rings,
deeds,
ownership?
I am a landlord, I think,
of the emotions,
just trying to collect my rents,
regularly.

You have what you were born with. No more.
How I have fought that rule;
and worshipped it.
The pain of life.
We are born
as diamonds
having to endure the world's
cutting us into shape
or we remain
undiscovered
like dirty chunks of rock.

I speak again
here
of myself,
not because I am different from you.
We were,
I think,
all intruders
to some measure
and try to create in our adult lives
a sense of mastery,
over our surroundings: the world no longer will just
"tolerate" us—
we will see to that.
We will be the owners,
the possessors,
the ones who must be petitioned, the landlords.

And it is understandable,
real,
a way of taking the past and thrusting it in a closet,
getting it out of sight;
but it breeds a kind of greed
that in its very rationality
can overtake us,
become impossible to purge. We can excuse it
too easily, can condone it,

can even use it as an excuse
to help other people.
But as it becomes insulated with reason and
understanding,
it grows and grows. The greater this need of possession,
of security, of insulation from the past,
the greater significance does that past itself
obtain.
You never lose the sense of being an intruder.
And what is more,
you cast everyone in your life into that role—
the intruder who's using your possessions,
the intruder who's taking up your time,
the intruder who's accidentally stealing your affections.

THE TURTLE

The turtle swims slowly,
leisurely.
On the volcanic ashland of the Galapagos
where the turtles weigh 200 pounds;
you could see one
move slowly
dragging trails to the middle of an island
where he finds fresh spring water;
you might see one pushing
for hours
against a deep rock
or a tree trunk
because the object was in his way
and it never occurred to him
to go around,
never occurred either
that he could not push over the object
if he just kept pushing
even if it took several
days.

The turtle carries everything he needs
with him,
except food and water;
he is a complete man of possessions;
no one ever intrudes on his house.
Not until death.
Stubborn,
slow,
unbelieving that the world
could defy him,
he is a survivor.
A creature so weak,
so vulnerable,
but somehow
inpervious.

If only life left us with metaphors.
But we are lucky if life
leaves us
with life.

How can we condemn
that greed then
which manifests itself as a survival force,
a desire to insulate ourselves
from onslaught,
to possess those things which keep us daily
from the edge of despair?
Only because there is no way to do it
without robbing our lives
of their reality.
Surrounded by possessions,
we become once removed from life.
Then life becomes once removed from us.
As if to destroy your car
is to destroy a piece of you;
to take away your house
is to take away the years of you that lived in it;

to take away your money
is to take away the character that earned it;
to leave you,
saying
maybe I couldn't do it again;
to take away your clothes
is to take away your image
as the world sees you;
to take away your jewels
is to remove your beauty.

All life then
but a little spark
that keeps the heart going back and forth
between the starting and finishing lines.
And you remove one possession at a time;
thus removing you.
How can we blame
a man for his greed, his desire
to own things that represent himself
and then to so value them
that the self is forgotten
as a little *a priori* consideration,
a guilty match
that started the whole Chicago fire.

But we are authors,
all of us,
concerned with beginning,
with making,
with sources and substance. And those possessions,
the objects of our desire for security
are results,
not causes,
in our lives. When we too much honor
them, we start weakening ourselves
and fear of loss
becomes even greater than the desire

for life.
A pistol shot in the head
when the '29 market crashes.
A slashed wrist
when the jewels are taken by popular revolt.
An alcoholic condition
when the house goes back to the bank.

The greed for possessions:
fear that we'll be left only with ourselves,
become intruders,
once more,
living in a world
that finds us a burden.
Greed.
Who cannot say it is not a survival trait?
Look how it keeps the evil alive;
look how early
good men die.
And I,
the author of all this,
the landlord of the emotions I call myself earlier,
giving up so much,
but wanting so much more.

How can I sign myself?
Other than as
another greedy man?
How can I sign myself,
sitting in someone else's chair,
fearing the opposite of this man
      even the world
fearing to buy my own chair?

Is there any place
that could take me beyond these concerns?

Yes.

An answer
could be in your hand,
your face,
your mustache
brushing my lips. My greedy desire
is not to possess you,
only to love you,
just to touch you,
old man,
Galapagos turtle,
intruder.
You,
landlord
of my heart.

GREED, Part 5

The Shark — Parents & Children

I can't swim.
I am afraid of water
    or
what lives in it.
I love the ocean.
I get seasick.
If I could choose one place in the world to live
it would be at the beach
even though
I can't swim.
I am afraid of water
      or
(fascinated by)
what lives in it.

I am trying to concentrate on my didactic feelings
about the shark.
From my encyclopedia I learn
about life
and as I read about the shark
my mind wanders/
                stream of consciousness
    the water
      our tears
      amniotic fluid
my own children — a son
              a daughter
lost to me
me lost to them
forever
unless perhaps some day this tiger shark
floats down some river,
a message in a bottle gets to them
tells them
how much
I love the world,

the people in it,
how much I
don't want any of
           them
to suffer
all the things I have had
to suffer.

Sacrifice.
That means giving up something.
No. That means giving up something which seems great
        in the eyes of the world
        in your eyes?
for something which seems
in a worldly sense
less
but in a spiritual sense
greater.
The idea is of spiritual returns.
Intangible ones.
I gave up my children when I was young
because I had no money,
no husband.
Children cannot understand or accept poverty
the way adults can.
They hate their parents,
but they need them.
Every child is damaged by his parents.
Every parent is damaged by his children.
Children are more damaged when they have only one parent
than two.
I gave up my children so they could have
better parents
and not have to suffer poverty.
I gave up my children so that I could have all my time and
energy to be a person/a poet.
There should not be any sacrifice here.
That the children had to give up me

was no sacrifice because they got a complete set of parents,
better than I
and will never have to suffer poverty.
They gave up something small to get something big.
They gave up something emotional to get something material.
That's not sacrifice. That's reward.
I gave them up to achieve my soul, my life.
That's not small.
That's something big for something small.
None of you will understand this.
Unless you have divested yourself of sentimentality.
And most of you haven't done that.
Sacrifice is sentimental.

* * *

Sharks are found in all seas
of the world & at
all depths.
        I dig down/ to all depths
the scuba diver,
the skin diver
        (that lover
         that black man
         who comes up out of my heart
         with a baby sand shark
                this funny face:
                it's no good to eat,
                won't hurt anyone
goes down/
        I come
   up
with memories like baby sand sharks
dangling in
my hands, wet, new born/ just caught
        all the ways that loving hurts people.
My parents
who could give me nothing

but piano lessons
who pulled me out
of their harmless genes

have I anything to
thank them for

but the gift of life?

This breath,
this water that runs silvery
thru my hair
glistening on my lips
that came out of my eyes
this ocean that holds my spongy brain.

I want to talk about
        the greed that makes a parent want a child.
        That makes a woman want to use her body
        as a stretched, swollen, lumpy pocket in an old
        worn coat,
    that makes a man want to see some squalling
    smelly inarticulate baby animal take his name
    and imitate his actions.

What is that greed?
That mirror.
That desire for repeating ourselves
stamping ourselves on the world? I see it
as an angel
or a devil
a salmon or a shark.
                      It could make
these same people
produce beautiful objects
benevolent institutions
or write books and religions.

                        But in most
it only produces
the common herd
                children
                            more likenesses
of ourselves.

I am not arguing.
to depopulate the world
by the way.
            Am rather saying
that some greed for our own existence
our identities
produces both children
and civilization.
But a human child stays at home
with his creator
too long.
Imagine
        if every novelist rewrote his book for 18 years,
        every architect re-designed his buildings for 18 years,
        a president spent 18 years rewriting a bill before trying
            to get it passed,
        a cook worked 18 years on the same ingredients.
Absurd?
But there our analogies could start working.
    I want to go back to my book about sharks.
The shark lacks bone. Its skeleton is cartilaginous.
It also lacks an air bladder.
Its skin is covered with scales.
It has several sets of external and internal teeth.
It is carnivorous.
Has a well developed sense of smell.
It is stupid.
The fins are valued for soups and as aphrodisiacs.
Its liver is a valuable source of Vitamin A.
According to fossil evidence
sharks are primitive creatures

                    Dogfish
                    Hammerhead
                    Macheral Shark
                    Monkfish
                    Porbeagle
                    Thresher Shark
                    Tiger Shark
                    Whale Shark
when I start listing beautiful names
it is because my own pain is so deep.

Do you know the story
of my life?
Everything is a distraction.
I am a fish swimming in mined waters.
I am a fish in water that has been torpedoed.
I am a fish in a volcanic ocean.

Oh, the detritus, the confusion, the noise, the floating anger.

I want to chronicle this story.
I have never told it before.
I wonder
if it is a story everyone knows?
One I tell,
inadvertently,
every day of my life.
I am arrested
by my fears, my stupidities, my failures,
and my attempt to turn these tormenting realities
into a structure of strength,
a moral argument,
a stern face.
Am I stupid, am I cruel, am I a shark too?
with a small brain, an instinct
for greed?
Am I the one thing man has to fear;

am I a long bloated fallen
scarred ugly metaphor?
Hurt
hurt
hurt
I have been so
hurt.
How can I talk about my hurt.
I went swimming in shark infested waters
    sharks exploding like waterlilies to the surface,
    sharks like airplane pilots,
    on fire,
    sharks like acid eating my throat:
    my throat
          and I lost my legs
          I lost my arms,
          they are ladders of shale and lime, my voice
          is deserting me. I cannot talk
          under the water
          of my tears.
          There are old bones. They are older than any
          survivor of slavery.
Greed. I am talking about wanting more than
you have earned.
More than your life can support.
More than your body can digest, use, tolerate,
sustain.

This greed makes a man desire to extend his
definitions
in the world
by having children,
by making them extensions of himself.

This greed makes a man afraid of living his own life, all by himself,
and gives him children to substitute for the areas of his life in which
he fails. This greed makes a man, fearing failure, offer to the world

these children as excuses, as hard work along the way, as digressions
from his real work, as responsibilities that give him a valid excuse for
not having the time or energy to succeed at the goals for himself.

(But what excuses do I practice?
What sharks live in my empty belly?)

Stop digressing,
I say to myself. Why aren't you saying
what you want to say? There's
no music here.
Only strong loud thuds that bang the piano keys,
crush the keyboard,
bloody.
Bloody fingers.
Smashed. No music. Sharks filling the water,
circling for my blood. The east river is in my house.
The ocean is in my ears.
The deaf man under my bloody face, my
hands, helpless, shame.
> The blood of shame.
> The blood of living without love.
> I am not noble.
> I am not strong.
> I did not give up my children for goodness; but
> because I was helpless,
> crushed, stupid,
> bloody, weak.
> And I would not criticize others now
> who are not good parents,
> who use their children as possessions,
> who disguise their own failures with the accomplish-
> ments of children,
> who don't want children and so compete with them and
> crush them,
> who make weaklings to prove their own feeble strengths,
> who try to validate their lives with carbon copies.

Forget all this. The bad bad parents.

Are there any good ones?
My grief is old and ugly.
The wounds on my belly
                —like them
                ugly wrinkled old lines.
Pain
pain
pain.
If
I say it again and again, will the pain
like sediment in the water
clear away
and leave me with a story I can understand?
A reality I can—

Stop talking.
You are blood
clouding the water.
You can only attract sharks.

Pain.
No man has wanted to spend his life with me.
The pain of sharks eating at my throat.
No man has asked me to share my life with him.
The pain of sharks eating at my lips.
No man has wanted to marry me.
The pain of sharks biting at my cheek.
No man has been willing to take care of me or give me a home.
The pain of sharks eating at my ridged, aching back.
Each vertebra a bullet. A lump of scar tissue.
A strength earned by sharks biting and making me
bleed.
      I could not stand up
                I grew new bones
I am a tower of ugly strength, this body
only the sharks have enjoyed.
No man has wanted my children.
Pain

pain.
The shame of being a woman
with a big belly
     and no man
     to claim the child.
Only the sharks.
Throw them my heart
as diversion.
The pain of my shark-eaten heart.
The pain of bleeding and being unnamed.

This could not be a statement about greed.
It is about pain.
My pain.
Pain
pain.
My weeping from
pain.
The greed I have tried to understand in others/
not those who feel pain
but those who create it.

And the pain
I know
my own children
my son
my daughter
must feel not knowing why they have different parents
than the ones they were born to.
They will trouble themselves with grief
asking why
over and over
their mother,
their father
did not want them. Searching for some secret flaw,
some insignificance which will torture them
at night.

Just as I torture myself again and again
with the question: what was wrong with me? Why
has no man ever wanted me
and my children,
even now
that I am old and past such desires,
when words are more to me
than flesh could ever be,
yet I
like every woman
must ask myself
those questions, and when I do
my shoulders lift out of the water
dazzled
surrounded
by the mouths waiting to tear apart
my flesh.
It is a cold and hungry world.
There is only one thing you can honor a man for:
transforming his suffering into something beautiful—
Beethoven
my inspiration
the only thing which forgives my fevers,
would not
however,
prevent a shark
from tearing any of us apart.
Yet I would prefer Beethoven
to a competing pair/   of teeth.
We are all sharks.
The only question will be
                    whose flesh
will we strip
bloody and raw
from the bones?
Will it be our children's
or our own

or some poor stranger who comes by
when we are hungry
and it is time
for another cold meal?

GREED, Part 6

Jealousy — A Confessional

> *This poem is dedicated to Humphrey Bogart in*
> *The African Queen who knew how to pick the*
> *leeches off. "Nasty things," he called them.*

They are black,
and they gleam like Steinways.

28 May 1970

Dear Diary:
For the past few months these feelings have been exploding inside me, giving me a sore throat with all the angry words I have held back and not said, giving me a sense of heaviness, as if my veins were gorged with blood or some poisonous liquid, and making people keep away from me for the angry things that have overflowed and poured out of me, despite my attempts to remain controlled.

These feelings are too immediate, intense, and especially too petty and mean to make poetry or art from. And I do not believe psychiatrists or religion help one much — at least not one like me who fights off all authority figures as if they were alligators trying to snip off an arm or leg.

The terrible thing about these feelings is that they have invaded both my personal and my professional life, and they are attacking me, like a school of sharks, all at once, in every vital area trying to destroy everything that is decent and generous and high-minded about me.

Those are qualities, by the way, that I've always prided myself on. Decency — behaving well and honestly, with fairness towards other people. And generosity — since I myself have been so afflicted by the stinginess of the world. And, of course, high-mindedness — why else have I lived a life with so few material or tangible rewards, other than that I believe in honesty and courage and virtue, will not be hypocritical for the small amounts of harmony it temporarily distills.

But now, this jealousy is sucking away at me, like leeches, and threatening to leave a poisoned, feeble animal behind. There is no woman I meet who I feel isn't trying to steal the man I love away from me. By being more beautiful. By acting more intelligent. By having more money or talent. There is no poet I meet who I feel hasn't stolen bread out of my mouth by winning a grant, a prize, a reading or recording that I didn't get. I never read a review any more without feeling that my work is more worth talking about than whoever is being reviewed. I never hear praise of anyone else without wanting to kill or destroy them. I see every wealthy person as having wealth I should have had. I see every married woman as a living symbol to remind me that I am unmarried and unmarriageable. I see every beautiful face as a reminder of my plain one. I see in fact anything which I have tried to associate myself with—even ideas—as my 33 year old possessions and begin to feel drained, sucked dry, leeched out, the minute anyone else participates even for a minute in them.

I guess jealousy must come out first, greedily narcissistically making a person or an intangible idea of something into a possession, and then having done so, constantly feeling that it will be stolen away from you. Sometimes, and this is when the jealousy is worst, it is something you have never had at all; but thought you deserved it more than whoever had it (an award, an honor, money, someone you love who doesn't love you?) and then the jealousy is rampant and unrelenting and it is like having leeches on every part of you, from the soft spots between your toes, to the inner fatty thighs, through the soft belly and armpits, to the neck, trying for the eyes, eager for the brain.

This is sheer confession, by the way. I am talking about it for one simple reason: so that you will know about it. And it is trying to kill me, and these may be my last words on the subject. There is no poetry for it. Those blood suckers have done their work inside this blood factory, and killed any of the energy that makes a beautiful song, lament, argument, narrative or portrait. I don't even ask you to forgive me or be indulgent. There is ugliness and madness here, and while these leeches are present, no decency can exist. Perhaps I believe in exorcism. Oh, obviously I do believe in exorcism or at least catharsis, and that is my purpose too in writing all this out. To clean myself out. To get rid of it. But I wonder? You've heard of people being operated on for cancer—the surgeon opening them up and seeing those deadly extra cells cropping out everywhere like friends at a surprise party—behind the chairs and sofas and pianos in a seemingly empty room.

Or have you ever opened a piece of fruit or an ear of corn and found it full of worms. And they wake me up in the middle of the night, as they did last night, screaming for blood. Leaving me bursting with some indefinable feeling and a need to scream very very loud.

This is not a sudden disease. One leech doesn't do you in. But something that builds. Something that is applied over and over. The "medicinal" leech that is applied each day—until too much blood is gone. So I know it didn't happen overnight. It's not like food poisoning that you can trace to one guilty piece of meat; a bubonic plague to some innocent rat harboring the lethal fleas. No. If it's hit me in epidemic proportion this year—this case of greedy hungry jealousy—then it's been there growing for a long time.

But I *can* pinpoint its power. I can tell you when those fires that burn as fever in me got inflamed and started that hard fast burning that leaves me pale and weak and petty—oh, so petty and mean and unworthy for the next few days.

I don't know why I'm putting all this down actually. I don't know why I'm confessing all these things to you. Oh yes, I said before that I believed in exorcism. And I'm trying to get rid of my demons. But why am I telling you? Why do I think you should be interested? Well, I guess I'm telling you because there can be no confession without an audience to confess to. Someone to hear you, to sigh for the human condition, be angry at evil, and then wave his hand in the air and feel that he knows more about life. I suppose I think you'll be interested because madness always interests other a bit and some of you probably will feel that I'm talking, even, about your own madness and wonder if perhaps I'll give you any insights into your own ways. Any answers. But I am angry at myself that I can't get this into lines, instead of sentences, that my metaphor of the leeches isn't more profound or inventive, that I don't have more images to dazzle you with, or more universal experiences to talk about. And I love ironies. So my favorite thing to do would be to write a long poem despising and putting down Pulitzer Prizes and then win one for it. But, critics, when you read this, I don't for once want you to review it; I want you to review yourselves and learn not about literature, but about life—how goodness, or the desire for it drives us mad. And, of course, I want you to reflect on those who are still sane—from innocence or evil. And think a while about them both—the innocent and the evil.

Last night: why did I wake up last night with a strange feeling—alone, wondering if you were with some other woman, having dreamed this:

> My mother was my husband's (in the dream) first wife. In real life I don't have a husband. In real life my mother has white hair. Had white hair at the age of 32 when I, her first child, was born. Her father, my maternal grandfather, had white hair at the age of 30. I am now 32, the age my mother was when I was born, and I have blond hair with a lot of silvery-grey strands in it. Anyway, in the dream, my mother had long silver-white hair, and when she died my husband scalped her and kept the long silver-blond hair in a wooden box. He took it out often during the dream, combed and admired it, and at one point, even, cut it. During the dream, there was a car ride in which someone was chasing us to prove that we had stolen a case of peas from the A & P. I was angry at my husband because he kept stopping the car to comb and admire my mother's scalp.

Anyway, I woke up suddenly thinking I must either call or write you, Tony, and demand 3 things. Fortunately I curbed myself, got a drink of water, read a John Cheever story, turned over on my belly, turned out the light, and made myself go back to sleep by thinking of all the different ways an ocean can look from a cliff-ish beach. I felt, when I woke up, however, that I had to demand three things from you. And, in spite of the favorable fact that I have not demanded them, they still haunt me. I felt I had to demand that you tell me what girl you had with you last February when I came to your apartment where we had lived together for a year and a half, after you had thrown me out a week before, saying you wanted to be alone. Remember when I came and found the upper dead bolt locked? Is that really the name of the lock I wonder—"dead bolt"—or did I make that up to fit my feelings? Writing a poem about that day—a good poem—has never exorcised the image of that girl's leather purse left on your couch, the closed bedroom door and the look on your face when I asked you if there was a girl in there. And it sometimes worries me so much, wondering who she was and why you wanted her and not me, that I can't move or think. Why didn't you want me? Why did you want her? I guess I had been dreaming, actually, that I came home and that dead bolt was on. I woke up being more jealous of that girl than of the fact that you had once married someone else.

The second thing I woke up feeling I had to demand from you, Tony, was the name of that blond girl whose photograph you had in your bedroom when we got back together this winter. The one you took with you to Vermont last summer and whom you must have treated as your girlfriend—am I anything more?—for a while. Why I want to know her name is a mystery even to me. Surely I don't want to go out and murder her, though at times I easily could. Why should I want to make her life miserable? That is past. You spend your time with me. But she is still, the idea of her is still, an affront to me. Someone you *preferred* to me. I could never feel this way about women you were involved with before I knew you. But this is different. You had thrown me out of your house. Out of your life. You had rejected me. And she is someone you took in preference to me. That will always be a memory that hurts.

There's the jealousy. You are, of course, not my possession, though I always think of myself as yours. Perhaps because I am a "possessed" woman and prefer to think of you possessing me than some devil. Even though you are not/cannot/I would not want you to be my possession, I suppose I think of love as possessing. And the idea that you let someone else possess you in preference to me drives me into a fury, as if someone had stolen one of my poems and said he had written it. There, you see. Petty. Small. Ungenerous. Besides the basic flaw of thinking of persons as possessions, the real human failing is being ungenerous with those possessions. How I hate myself for that. Pettiness is a trait I cannot tolerate. It is the source of evil. Not power, as some people say. Power only augments evil. Pettiness creates it.

And the third thing that I was going to demand of you was that you marry me. But I have no rights there. That you care for me, I know. What difference should it really make if the world knows it or not?

For me, crazy and mixed up on the subject of possessions marriage is the symbol that a man cares enough for a woman to let the world know about it. Anything other than marriage is their private arrangement, their temporary, though often passionate or fine, feeling for each other. When you marry, you say to everybody, this woman is the one I prefer. Again, here is a pettiness on my part. Why should I care if the world thinks no one cares for me? Is it that I feel so small and insignificant that I cannot imagine anyone thinking that anyone else could care for me?

Well, anyway, I didn't call you or write a letter demanding any of those things. And that is why I must write them as part of a confessional this morning, and while I know it is still petty and weak of me to need to do this, at least it is not so very ungenerous and indecent of me as burdening you with the responsibility for my torment would have been.

There is a man I've met a few times, actually whom I like. The idea of his money has sucked at me in every spot until I am weak and foolish on the subject of money; or money and people with it; or money and artists; or maybe it's money and me. Anyway, I am terribly jealous of this man's income and spend hours wondering about how to make money myself. And yet, it seems obvious that money is not my main concern or I would not be so careless with it, nor would I have chosen to become a poet—surely a profession which never creates millionaires. The idea of a man, heir to millions, who has a $300,000 a year income and who writes poetry which doesn't deal with what surely must be the paramount experience of his young life—what it means to be wealthy—angers me. In my jealousy I see him with his young, unformed poetry taking away my jobs, my reputation, my publishers, winning prizes I never win, and being paid more for poetry readings than I am. In the abstract, or when I see him, I like him; perhaps am even a little in love with him. But the vision of his $300,000 lowers down over my head like a safe coming out of a 10th story window, crashes on me, and I feel the little mouths of those leeches biting down, beginning to drain my color, taking all my courage and energy from me. Making me into a bitter, aging, nasty woman.

I am very melodramatic. I see myself hanging on a cross, with nails gouging out the thick flesh of the feet and pulling through the bloody tendons and delicate bones of the hands. "Poetry where are you," I say, feeling that most of the men and women who call themselves poets are idle dumb fools with tin ears and petty lives. I hate myself for being so small, so unfeeling, and for smiling at these people weakly instead of snarling, if indeed that is really the way I feel. My sins get larger every day. I take a breath and realize I am not only mean and ungenerous but also a hypocrite about it. I start with lack of generosity, an unwillingness to appreciate others, descend to pettiness in making nasty comments about them or their lives and works, and end, compounding my ugly greed, by being hypocritical and smiling at them when they pass by. These are sins nothing can absolve me from. Ones that can only be mended by becoming first an honest person, and then trying to regain some of my original generosity and decency towards others. But is there any left in me? Or have I been sucked dry? Each year of poverty has taken its toll.

Each year when I was ignored and others far less capable or interesting were praised. Each year I applied for something and my forms were returned with a printed rejection. Each time the man I loved betrayed me with another woman or refused to marry me or threw me out, saying he wanted to be alone. Each time I was scorned in some way, when something, as I saw it, which belonged to me was taken away and given to someone else.

A good man is one who sees no cause for bitterness in this. Who does not find himself demeaned or hurt by such things. But what is it that protects him, keeps him whole, gives him transfusions of plasma to replace his evaporating blood?

Perhaps faith in himself? A belief that art or love or anything valuable and beautiful is beyond the temporal?

Whatever it is, it is feeble and ill in me. I am a transplanted tree, elm, oak, some hard wood, at the droopy stage. Will my melodramatic roots, that in my former location nourished me, take hold in this new space and grow?

I cannot continue this confessional. Here is a poem:

THAT DELICATE REPTILE

There is a small pink coral snake
like the ring of a Countess
curled up
in my brain, eating it away.
I keep finding real reasons
like birds that fly out of a tree, a cloud of them, when you walk
under it,
for why I am angry,
hurt,
unsatisfied,
but all the time it is that snake eating morsels
of the brain, expanding
a little to take
a bigger place there,
sliding his body, with each scale rippling
                like a blood transfusion
to move
into a newer
thicker
coil.   My neck aches
unbearably; to carry anything
is torture, though I do it out of a sense of
human responsibility; when I tilt my head,
I lose my balance
and feel as if I had been eating snakes.
Oh, that small dainty reptile
that bracelet
coral as a rabbit's eye
the size of a thermometer,
is slowly replacing my brain. The angers I feel
are poisonous and bitter;
the love I feel unsteady and frightened as though
treachery were a norm;

and these pains through the trunk of my neck
penetrating the backs of my ears,
remind me
of that delicate snake
which has lodged itself there.
I have always been
a good neighbor;
but his eyes tell me,
gleaming like two pinholes in a dark curtain
that he does not much care for
old rules.
I sit down to smoke, but a nudging
behind my ears
signals
that if I were prudent
I'd stop.
I try to quote a line of poetry. Something about
good fences
and realize it doesn't apply.
His being in my brain
it being his living room, so to speak —
I wonder now
about his name.
But
this is a little late
for such preliminaries. I sit still
and wonder
when will he decide
to make himself known
to the world?

Will I,
do you suppose,
have my choice
of being deadly
or
dead?

GREED, Part 7

Self-Righteousness

"Pride goeth before a fall,"
repeated my mother
self-righteously to her children. "Pride
goeth before a fall,"
I repeated to myself,
though it was much more likely
I would stumble and fall
because I was near-sighted and couldn't see,
much more likely I would fall
because the porch steps were broken
or because I was clumsy and ashamed of my body
and afraid of my life.
But I was different,
quiet,
my face turned red
when spoken to,
                    and I was proud,
proud, proud,
like some beautiful creature deep in the ocean,
dug into the underwater caverns
moving slowly
through gorgonians, sea fans,
spreading over the breathing walls,
aloof,
unexploited.
I was a little ocean named Diane,
a coral reef,
a sea anemone,
a chambered nautilus,
glowing with possibilities no one knew.
"Pride," my mother
would whisper,
as I played the piano,
as I sped through school books with lightning speed,
oh the light of the underwater
world,

glinting,
reflected, inside my own head I was
the Lion Fish of Saudi Arabia,
swimming slowly through the Red Sea,
long spines,
like files,
or the rails from spiral iron stairs,
stick up in a fan,
a mane,
over my body.
Their poison is more deadly
than the bite of a cobra,
my fins are angry too,
slowly they open and shut,
seeming to breathe,
and I move wherever I want to go,
unharmed and beautiful
because
deadly.   The Lion Fish
born in the constellation of that roaring beast,
blundering through the summer sky,
pausing on my own porch steps to hear my mother say,
"pride
goeth before a fall,"
and looking grimly at me,
saying she hoped my life was better than
hers,
    pride
she seemed to whisper,
making me hunch my already-round shoulders,
lowering my eyes,
my face turning as red as the Lion Fish
a kind of lobster king,
arms stiff with anger
when anyone looked at me.
What destiny is there
in the ocean;

it follows me,
the fire,
moving through water.
Pride holds my tongue,
makes me stammer,
gives me insufficient wit;
pride makes me grovel in shame when I see the
pride in others that is
ugly,
the self-righteous smugness
of safety, assurance,
the feeling that there are no mistakes;
pride makes me immodest when I compare myself
to less beautiful,
less deadly
creatures of the sea
                          even the sharks steer clear of me . . .
But pride is not
a source of shame,
of ugliness
or hurt
in human lives. Pride is
what gives us dignity,
even when we fall.
Oh, my mother, whispering to me,
who knows why,
making me ashamed of anything I could do,
making me afraid to assert myself
or to claim my rights.
Pride
is not
to be ashamed of.
                    But it is related to that deadly Lion Fish
we should all fear;
self-satisfaction,
self-righteousness,
smugness
and the anger that goes with it,

the willingness to say you are right
everyone else wrong.
                    There burn the fires of the Inquisition.
Self-righteousness makes truth,
honesty, goodness,
honorable actions—all of them
the victims of themselves. The fires that burn in me
when I am right
and the whole world is wrong,
when, in spite of temptation and torture
I have done the decent good thing
and everything else around me is corrupt
and corruptly perpetuating itself,
and I see this
and I start burning inside
with my rightness,
at that point I am ready to
forego
everything truth, honesty, goodness, and honorable actions
stand for,
and be carried away into the anger of the
righteous,
and from there,
comes vanity,
selfishness,
uncharitableness,
the angers that feed vengeance.
From purity, the transposition to corruption,
and all because the world does not often
honor
goodness
and unless we do, so much,
in our own minds,
then leading a good life
will make us angry
vengeful men.

Mother,

you whisperer of mottos
and guidelines,
you painful lesson in innocent evil,
it is not "pride that goeth before"
all my falls
but pride in what is right and good that picks me up
when I do fall;
pride, dignity,
faith in myself that allows me to realize how badly I
have acted some times
and not to be callous about changing
for the better.
You,
you reminder in the dark
of your own failings and hoping I would fail
too, you weak plunderer of children
in the name of goodness
and righteousness, with your "pride goeth before a fall"s,
and your "cleanliness is next to godliness"es and
other more secret doctrines
        like "lay low for meddlers"
        the poetry of childhood,
smugly sitting there feeling
the world was doing you in,
self-righteously sitting there
hoping they would martyr you and you would be innocent,
oh the perils of perverse Christianity,
welcoming grief and oppression
rather than learning to fight them and only to submit
when there were no other alternatives.
Oh you false teacher,
letting me think if I were honest
and clean and straight,
the world would just be all right,
and that if it weren't I could sit righteously
in my chair of innocence and look back
at it
and somehow triumph.

But the world only admits it is wrong,
when you make it admit it is wrong;
and where is the poetry in that?

I have never been under the sea,
though photographs serve nicely to prick and pull
at my imagination.
This Lion Fish, which I have only seen on film,
is a magnificent creature,
living in very deep waters,
and it is a testimony to my history
that poisonous living things fascinate me,
the beautiful fin-spikes this fish wears like a mane,
the knives of 90 feet below,
with their Borgia touch,
what I would give to float so serenely through the world,
radiating the power that poison gives.
For the poison I know in my life
is poison that poisons me; the fire I know burns me
up; waters drowns me and my fingers are not ice to others,
but their very touch freezes me.
I have walked so innocent,
for so many years,
and it is my own innocence that turns on me.
I have walked straight and honestly for so many years,
and it is my own honesty that
turns on me.
The men I loved so single-mindedly, so passionately,
so without guile —
they were frightened and angered and burdened by that very
single-mindedness, that passion,
that honesty.
The world I love,
full of artists, listening to their own sirens,
wailing in caverns under the water or
in a drum that beats behind some impenetrable wall,
they who roar like lions and live in the back of printing presses,
or those whose paint brushes are soaked

with sunlight, painting canvases with invisible elements
of piracy, the rare spices and gold brought from great distances,
that world I have asked so much of:
purity,
honesty,
recognition of true beauty,
art rather than deception,
imagination rather than guile,
that world where I've walked
worked
never trying to deceive,
always trying to give fair measure for what I take/

but to then expect that world to be as straight
and simple, as I see myself,
when it's older and more complex and
considerably different
from me—
a simple notion,
one that innocence can support.
But when innocence goes,
   —to school or to work—
simplicity is no substitute for intelligence.

My mother made me a breeding ground for
self-righteous anger.
It fermented in me like beer in an oak keg.
It ripened like Camembert,
it rose like yeast in good bread.
But I did not become a good meal of bread and beer and cheese.
I became an angry woman,
innocent only in my foolishness,
and the anger and vengeance nearly burned me up.
Not one corrupt hair of anyone I hated, or any air-conditioned
room of any falsely administered institution
caught on fire, got singed,
or even felt my own heat.
I was a bird caught in an oil slick from industrial nations.

I was a fish contaminated with 10 parts of mercury per 1000
                                                    in my guts.
I was a child playing in a field sprayed with parathion.
I was the side of a hill wrecked with open-pit mining.
I was Joan of Arc, a stubborn girl burned wastefully at the stake.
I was not a reformer.
I was not the reliever of corruption.
I was not even the means of success,
nor will I ever be.
My angers come from having lived as I was taught
and not feeling the world honors or
rewards me for any of my decency.
This anger has made me hard
and harsh
vain
unable to accept other people's success,
unable to believe any one else is honest,
    though in my angers I have learned to be
    dishonest,
unable to think of intrinsic rewards and merits,
taught me to be greedy and foolish and most of all,
bloodthirsty for vengeance on all
who have won false rewards.
The self-righteoous executioner, I stand ready
to chop heads, hang weak men
and electrocute my detractors. There is no virtue here,
where my mother's anger burns,
whispering "pride goeth before a fall," and holding out
an ancient foot to trip all who pass before me.
Not pride,
not pride
which may heal us
and take us away from false issues
and impossible goals.
That Lion Fish,
that natural arsenal,
equipped for destruction —
self-righteousness,

the greedy thought that when you are right
you can burn others for their wrongness;
it is a fire that could destroy
the world.
It takes poets and holy men with it,
along with philosophers, scientists, parents,
and statesmen.
The mad bombers.
The Wars to End all Wars.
Remember the Lion Fish from the Red Sea—
its beauty
its poison,

why should we touch it?

GREED, Part 8

The Desire To Be What One Is Not
While Clinging To What One Is

The Darker Wishes — To A Machine Who Wishes To Be A Man
The Sad Beautiful Music Of The Poetry Robot

in the cover of his darkness,
his owl
a bird of purity and wisdom
sits in a white wood, speckled with the deep soft feathers of
perfection.
"Who, who am I?" he asks
in the voice of a singer,
in the voice of an ugly man who loves beauty,
in the voice of a man who has lost everything
      honor
      money
      his wife
      his children
      his mind
           even
in some deep wood
where only those with the eyes of snakes, who hold the broken
   wind
in their pockets
can survive.
This owl
with the cloak resembling leaves, twigs,
his beak and claws red from the meek animals he needs to live on,
and his amazing voice,
this owl pretends to speak in the language of men
asking profound questions,
but he is the bird of deception,
the bird of that saddest of all creations,
the intelligent machine,
so perfectly made he can long for only one thing;
the cliché of science fiction

and modern life,
he was programmed to do everything but make mistakes
and thus by definition
he is no man,
no poet,
no sufferer
in this common rapacious world.
Whatever he is
is different,
apart,
beautiful
perhaps
in its very
inhumanity.

        Metaphors,
        I kiss you goodbye
        for a while
        and will talk about my own perceptions,
        angers,
        and even the admiration I feel for the beautiful
        scoundrel.

        There is a waitress at the coffee shop of the
        Holiday Inn in Corpus Christi, Texas, who if she
        had not been born Mexican in a Southern town, near
        the border, poor, and without ambition, would
        have quite a different life.
        Her hands are valentines serving my coffee. In
        her face, reside the petals of oleander & azalea.
        She walks like the wind in palm trees or a beautiful woman's hair. But she will always serve coffee
        to fat salesmen and dentists, and when she is finished talk to the short heavy Mexican bellhop. I
        ask myself, often, about that Christian proposition,
        "To those who have much, more shall be given; and
        to those who have nothing, even that shall be taken
        away."

> I would like to marry my Body-of-Christ waitress
> to the singer of dark sad music, who uses the owl
> to represent himself, and who has always walked
> through the world whistling a golden piccolo that
> disarms his listeners. I would like to give her
> some of his luck and even things out, for I am al-
> ways greedy to play god, but that is not what life
> is about.

The Poetry Robot.
He says everything beautifully.
He says (and will sue me for quoting,
but they are such beautiful words I cannot resist)
> "I give up my heart which is a burning apple.
>   I give up my arms which have wanted to leave me anyway."

and speaks of
> "the green field where cows burn like newsprint,"

and
> "The glass cloud in the shape of a heart,
>   the owl arranging all of the night,
>   the sleep of dresses on the warm bodies of women,
>   the applauding wind."

His words have always been polished,
as if he pulled emeralds out of the mountains,
already cut and in Tiffany settings.
The natural jewel,
the naturally beautiful and perfect jewel-maker.
How we all admire his glitter.
And if we are wise,
we *will* admire the perfectly made products
of fine and sophisticated machines.

But pick and choose.
Robot or Man. Machine- or hand-made,
you cannot have both.
Greed, I keep reminding you,
is the failure to choose. The unwillingness to pick one thing over
another. Wealth or simplicity; you cannot have both. Accord,
agreement, harmonious relations with others or your honesty; you

cannot have both. The
telling of the truth
is not beautiful; does not make people feel good.
I do not think any alternative is absolutely right or wrong.
I do know that it is absolutely wrong not to commit yourself
to one alternative or the other.

And today I speak of this dark and handsome bird,
this singer of sad songs,
the Poetry Robot,
the mechanical Golden Nightingale
(but he comes in many other disguises, my friends),
because he is singing a new song this year,
stolen from another bird,
the song of his frailty and his humanity.

He sings the song of a man bereft of fortune.
I know singers with one eye,
men with no livers left in their bodies,
men who will never have women in their lives,
women whose children were given away to strangers,
black men who will not ever know the dignity of being taken
   for granted,
and those whose lives are spent in jail.
They are singers of sad desperate and beautiful songs,
not so perfectly made
but poignant in their human sacrifice and misery,
deep in their knowledge of life.
Their suffering sometimes carves out magnificent language,
but it is never the simple beautiful artful language of the Poetry
Robot, the man who cannot speak an ungraceful line.
But he has cheated us
and so I am complaining.

Surely art can be made from all forms of humanity.
Surely the golden song of the perfect man
is no less sweet
than the sad human voice of suffering.

How can you not know that,
you Robot programmed to know everything?

You fraud,
you golden boy who is good at everything,
whose handsome face has appeared in fashion ads,
whose wife is a sweet noble intelligent loving lover and friend,
whose children are gifted,
whose ability to make money will never be questioned,
whose speaking wins you friends in every place,
whose books will always be published,
you who can do what you decide to do at any given time,
you fraud,
singing now of having nothing,
of giving all away,
and saying your world is nothing. If your world is nothing, man,
then there is no world that is anything.
Be honest, don't
tell us that life is sad
even for those who do not feel. That is only talking.
Talk to us of the owl
who asks you questions in the night
and tell us of the long perfect nights when there is no fear or hurt
to invade them.
Do not apologize for your perfections
or lie about them — they fade as you do;
say you're sorry for what you do not possess:
> a sense of your own good fortune and the willingness to
> rejoice in it;
> an understanding that if you sense misery in the world
> others must be dying of it;
> your unwillingness to use that beautiful music to
> soothe the sick and the dying.

I met a woman this week,
who made me praise my own normalcies.
For her, speaking was like running through the blades of a
windmill.

Her voice was like dragging a piece of metal under your car.
Her face contorted when she spoke
as if someone were electrocuting her for each syllable,
and when she ate, the food hung out over her mouth
moving like garbage in a river.
She walked as a bird would try to fly with a broken wing.
Yet she insisted on leading a real life,
going places,
talking to people,
writing poetry, longing for the language that falls cleanly out of
    you
like ripe plums off a tree.
Oh, you hypocrite,
don't you see that there is nothing noble in suffering?
That some suffering is every man's measure
and his only nobility comes from
seeing it through, living it out,
and transcending it; coming above it?
Do you think a man is noble for being beaten,
for starving,
for being unjustly persecuted,
for being physically tortured or losing everything he loves?
You, who have never suffered any of these things—
surely, you cannot be so foolish
as to wish to?
But the humanity of knowing the struggle
and any nobility that comes from surviving it,
that is what a mechanical bird cannot know.
My god, man,
you are privileged and above us.
We work
for what you have.
There may be a time when the world strikes you down too
and delivers no mercy.
Do not cultivate that time or long for it.
To do so is the opposite of what all life and religion
what philosophy and art
are about.

Sing
sing
sing
your perfect and harmonious songs.
Once you are honest about it,
even I with my torn body and painful memories
will listen.
It is the songs we want to hear after all.
And beauty is different, as each man finds it.
Give us your own,
tall handsome American and chrome.
Don't fall down,
or we'll kick you, where you lie.
Remember the fate of machines when they break down.
And we are always looking for new models.
Be yourself, #124966. And we will always
preserve you
for your integrity.

What is a philosopher?
    He is a man who gives no one the benefit of the doubt.

What is the artist?
    He gives us something beautiful from the darkness.

What is failure?
    The man who cannot live his own destiny.

These are the concerns
of us all
as we struggle with our own failures
and deceits.

GREED, Part 9

Introduction

Living from day to day is a series of compromises that must be made by every human being. To feel that in some way you are above having to bow down to those compromises is a kind of greed which often makes you long for death, which can be a kind of purity or relief from those human situations where you cannot always do as you believe, cannot have the life you believe is honest or correct or right; that to stay alive is to give up your standards or compromise them in exchange for life. In this poem, I try to address the destructive part of myself, a part I think every honest person has in himself, and to use the legend of Sylvia Plath, a poet who felt compelled to kill herself as a symbol for that alter ego, that Diane who could not or might not feel that when her husband leaves her and the world does not honor her and she cannot have or do the things she wants to do with her life, that she might in desperation be forced to take her own life.

This poem is a protest against the deception of that sense of purity, that greed which does not allow us to accept life on its own terms and which makes us feel as if we cannot summon the strength to go on in the face of life's afflictions. We all have them, by the way, and I don't for a moment feel that this poem is in any way personal, tho it is written in the most personal terms. If there is anyone who has not felt these things, he is either dishonest with himself or has so far had such a charmed life that I would be loath to believe it were true.

I would like to say that I feel that many people will read this poem wrongly if they think I wrote it in order to talk about Sylvia Plath. I wanted to use her legend as a symbol and nothing more in the poem. I wanted to make a public statement that I feel she succumbed to a terrible temptation which faces us all; this does not lessen her work in any way but it does make her a symbol for the weak, the destructive, the alien purist in all of us which is not a viable product of human evolution. My poetry is an attempt to define the world in humanitarian terms; to embrace both the honest and the compassionate because it is love and truth together which will save us/ not love alone; certainly not truth alone. The poet, as everyman, must have them both. His vision must hold that greater reality.

In this poem, I wanted to do several things at once: to make a statement to the world that I would not ever kill myself, no matter how much of myself felt compromised by the world; to sing a song for love and beauty in the face of sad truth; and to make the male chauvinists of the world stop comparing me to Sylvia Plath — as if all women of the world who write well must be similar. I don't know that the reader ever has to honor the purposes of the writer, if for no other reason than that we seldom really know what we're doing when we are creating a poem — it being one of those dark and desperate journeys. But if you are a reader who cares about my reasons for writing the poem, then I am happy to have shared my sense of them. May the poem in some way speak for you too.

The Water Element Song For Sylvia

> *for Sylvia Plath, a beautiful poet,
> and my friends, Kathy Saltonstall,
> J.J. Wilson, and the Martins*

The fish
perhaps they are alewives
lie gasping
and dying on the edge of the lake.
The lake itself is choking
and turning into a swamp.
For 33 nights I have lain on the edge
of this decadent body of water
and asked myself questions.
For as many days
I have counted my attributes
and cultivated my serenity;
and now has come the time for explanation,
definitions being past
and formed by life itself,
character and blood taking their miserable toll of lives,
and I have wept silently
and spoken angrily to empty rooms
and tried to resist pain without blunting my other feelings.
Thus, I feel I must speak of, about, and to Sylvia,
who stuck her head in a gas oven
out of a similar despair,
who wound two silver clocks at once
and found her hands broken under a handkerchief,
whose mouth hovered over a canyon in the West on a hot day
and found refreshment near Eastern jack-in-the-pulpits.
A river took her to breakfast.
She was a girl carrying the wind in her arms.

And I must speak of her beauty
and why she died,
breaking her own haunting words, like crackers into soup,

the breath, a thick silver spoon,
melting away in steaming liquid
and my urgency
is deep
and for myself,
a rough fish eating up the bottom of a lake,
a pledge, an affirmation, and a surly chin stuck out
at the world,
announcing my intention to survive.

Sylvia,
you fine-grained piece of white bread,
you piece of lace in an attic dress,
you crystal glass in a beanery,
you satin slippers worn to hike through a muddy wood,
you deserved so much
and got so little,
or were so mistakenly used,
as many of us are.
But in a classic manner
you died in order not to perpetuate
this commonness.
So this is my day to affirm my survival
and my commonness.
I am thick Polish rye bread,
I am homespun muslin,
I am stoneware,
I am a pair of wellingtons,
I can/I will survive
whether the man I love, who makes me calm on a windy day,
goes away or not.
I wont wont wont
die
even for poetry.
My children I have already given away,
and their lives are better without me.

For a woman

there is only one thing which makes sense:
a man who loves her faithfully & keeps her warm at night.
If he goes, her life does not go,
but it becomes a book with none of the pages in the right order.

Listen, Sylvia, you beautiful red & bloody tulip in a hospital
   room,
I know how you felt,
how the weight of days without your husband was like steel
   bearings on the eyelids,
I know how his denials & betrayals
made you feel your body was an empty stained test tube.
I know how you counted your jam jars in the middle of the night
waiting for his footsteps.
I know how his gravity pulled on you like a diesel truck attached
   to yr lip,
how, like a planet pulled out of its orbit
by another body's perturbations,
you were flung out into empty space
and could not survive its long night of outer darkness.
But I wont wont wont
die,
even for purity.

Sylvia, I want you to know what happened after you died —
      poets wept with one eye & laughed with the other,
      knowing you would no longer be there to astonish them
         with yr beautiful words,
      your husband took another wife and left her to gas
         herself also.
      publishers and relatives cleaned up on your dead sales,
      for everyone buys the book of a suicide,
      Sylvia, they all loved you better dead
      without your feelings there to chide them for lack of
         humanity,
      they all could talk about you when dead,
      and not be contradicted by life.
   Oh, Sylvia, I will never give any of them

    those satisfactions:
        no one will gloat over my body and say, "What a pity
          she didnt
live/
she might have been a great poet,"
no one will get the chance to be dramatic & remorseful
about not loving me enough,
they will have to prove their feelings while I'm living
or eat their own shit instead of shoveling it onto my
    grave,
no publisher or relative will clean up on my dead
    royalties because
I'll be living
and a man's work is as good when he's living as when
he's dead/
I dont want to flutter the pulse of the best-seller list
just because I'm a corpse,
and no mustached man will go to talk
late at night in bars about how wonderful I was/ he'll
    have
to prove it to me now
while I'm living.
I wont wont wont
die,
even for poetry.
Oh, no, Sylvia, they all stepped in
with their meanness and got fat on it
when you killed yourself
and I am too spiteful,
too angry,
too nasty to let the world
hypocritically walk on me.
If they want to slander me,
malign me,
treat me brutally,
or use me,
they'll have to do it in public
and with my sharp tongue

very much alive and chiding them
every minute of the way.
You might say I'm too bitchy,
my fiber's too common,
I'm peasant bread, not a delicate white roll.

When I think how many times
they have pushed me
and how close I have come to the cupboard of cyanide
I tremble with rage
at those persecutors.
Anger, anger, anger, I say,
rescue me:
let me fight:
Fatigue, do not cement me & throw me in the river;
Humiliation, if I lose what I love, do not cover my face with a
    black hood,
Sadness, do not crust me with the soot of your windows.
I wont wont wont
die,
for anyone's pleasure.

* * *

Here is our problem, Sylvia:
how to feel enough anger to survive
and yet not to spoil one's ability
to love,
how to love,
open oneself up,
be free,
and not be destroyed.
Is love always a body climbing over a
forbidden wall with a spotlight & machine gun on it?
Is honesty always suicide?
Would we all die like you,
if we were honest?

* * *

One pond
with one white duck
on a grey green day,
the waters muddy, not glassy & blue as I remember
the Pacific from my childhood.

And now a flock of ten white ducks
arranged like a slender skiff
moving in unison
as all the drops of water
make rhythmic formations & move
like one wave.

Now
two wild coots,
their heads black, bodies brown and streaked with white,
come,
red-winged blackbirds and crows
flying overhead,
all life seeks to perpetuate itself,
the birds spending their lives
searching for food
never storing
building new houses each year
life being a day-to-day and never-ending search,
only we humans taking time out to wonder
whether we want to go on.

Sylvia, our brains got too big,
our feelings are ripe apples all over the
many-limbed body
ready to fall off,
ready to be shaken off,
leaving an empty tree.
Simple apple tree,
you can lose your fruit, your leaves,
live through winter,
and be another tree next spring, summer & fall.

Your beauty is
that simplicity,
that dumbness,
that insensitivity to pain,
that inability to think about pain,
that lack of need for a complex & changing identity.
There are schizophrenics, I think,
madmen who try to turn themselves
into trees
who stand for hours
holding their two meager branches out
hoping only to stand there through the seasons
being only trees
never having to come to terms with
knowledge or failure,
betrayal, or deceit,
one's own anger at inhumanity.
Sylvia,
with your tongue of bellflowers & chicory,
wearing an apron of bees,
your white ankles like plover breasts flashing among field grass,
Sylvia, whose father called you a kitchen match & struck you to
    light up his pipe,
Sylvia, whose mother used you as a needle to sew the family
    shrouds,
Sylvia, whose husband was the claw of a bear
and whose hand stole the honey under that apron of bees,
Sylvia, whose children were a cloud of gnats stinging you around
    the
eyes and mouth, irritating you when you wanted to read or speak,
oh, Sylvia, who lived in constant terror
of being ignored or left behind by the one man you loved,
Sylvia, whose life was like mine,
with its baby hands asking for love
and being slapped by fathers, mechanics & woodsmen,
whose fatigue is from trying to hold a house of bricks with no
    mortar
together —

             as love & being loved
             can hold our lives together
             strong & sound
             in any weather —
Sylvia,
I wont wont wont
go the way you did;
I wont die for love, poetry, truth, or a man who betrays me;
my grandparents were potato farmers
and I have a bit of the simple potato
in me.
I have been a tree in winter,
and I did not scream when the birds
flew out of my hair.

Living from day to day is a humiliating effort.
And for those of us
whose dignity
is like shoes to wear on a long walk,
the bare bleeding feet of our failures
can give infection, gangrene, loss

How can we recognize our failures
and not feel sorry for ourselves?
And what feeling
is less imbued with dignity
than self-pity?

Sylvia, you would not fall into that
weeping well
of abandoned women,
so you floated away down some other river.
But I wont go with you:
             you, ring-necked loon,
             beautiful thin-noted flute,
             cup of Li Po's wine,
             girl with butterflies tattooed on your palm.
Your purity

which is a kind of poetry
is not real
not human
and if my life & the pains I have taken with it
are to mean anything,
I want them to speak for love,
for strength,
for surviving pain and using the knowledge
of it
to be compassionate to others.

I am as thin as a sheet of cellophane
this year.
I have no more innocent resistance.
I am dry and almost past tears.
So,
while I do not admire them
I will cling to my flaws:
> my easy anger,
> my selfish refusal to give that one possession I have left
>   (my life)
> away,
> and my spiteful desire to be alive
> to see my enemies suffer the natural consequences of their
>   own
> meanness, stupidity, & inhumanity.

Sylvia, I wont wont wont die.
I will not give anyone the pleasure
of my voluntary death,
tho it would be a relief to get it all
over with,
not to be alive in case the man I love so much
leaves me again,
not to be here fighting the battles of honesty & historical
  confusion,
not to have to suffer being alone or rejected or poor one more
  time,

I will go on even if I shred my own thin cellophane self ragged
in my sleep at night
because I want to believe
this pain & suffering have meant something,
that I can inspire someone to love me
long and faithfully,
and that my words, my life, may give someone
else
courage to go on.

I wont wont wont die
even for relief.
I wont let the other poets cry with one eye and laugh with the
　other
or relieve anyone of my searching hard but honest questions
　about them.
I wont wont wont
die
and let the world off easy.
Love is fighting the battle,
even when you think you might lose.
I will go on,
for love is the water that cannot be used up,
though it be transformed
　　　　　from lake
　　　　　to swamp,
　　　　　to sweat,
　　　　　to tears,
　　　　　to bloody underground stream.
Sylvia
when you are dead
no one really weeps for you;
they weep for themselves.
Sylvia,
this fish wont die
in the gasping lake today.
Water is life.
Water

is
life,
     in any
     form.

GREED, Part 10

A Note

Because this part of GREED, which was/is to be about love, sex, romance was not only conceived but begun, I have not wanted to close out the number or assign it to another part of GREED, even though "Part 10," finally, will probably never be finished.

I conceived of the poem as a long work, something like *Paterson,* written partly in prose, partly in my own poetic voice, the prose part to be in the form of letters, primarily letters to men I was interested in as recipients of my love, sex or romance. I began to think of these men as characters in an allegorical way—the Woodsman, the Motorcycle Betrayer, the Dean, the Cowboy. And, at a certain point, I began to consider using some of their letters as well as my own, for they were often elegant and interesting. At that point I began to have all the problems of a fiction writer. Was I going to invent names for the characters? Was I going to invent a story line? How was I going to edit my letters? Were all the poems to be contained in the letters? If I didn't change names, would I be sued? Even if I did change names, would there be problems?

During the early seventies I was writing many poems in the context of my letters, and as I was publishing a book of poems a year, I was syphoning off the poems from these letters to use in my collections of poetry. This brought up another problem. If most of the poems were already published, would there really be a reason to republish them in the matrix of the letters?

When I married my second husband, Michael, I more or less stopped the whole project, though I still thought I would someday "revise" what I had and make it "Part 10." But I remained stumped about what to do, and perhaps lost some of my zeal as I realized that the work would be more like an epistolary novel, as I envisioned it, than a poem.

Finally, I have reached a point where I do not have the same spontaneous relationship to letter-writing that I did in the seventies, and so when my papers went to a university archive, I sent along the manuscript which was the nucleus of "Part 10." But I still retain the option in my mind to complete it someday. For that reason, I insist that the text of *THE COLLECTED GREED: Parts 1–13* not close its ranks, and that "Part 10" be left open.

GREED, Part 11

Power

> dedicated to C.B. who wants it so badly, and to all the astronomers
> looking for new worlds, hoping to relieve us of one final fight
> over this tiny foolish one

I am no expert
(tho I admire them)
on either owls or eagles,
powerful, big birds of prey,
heavy as mahogany tables,
sitting,
watching,
circling above the world,
waiting to see/ to capture/ to kill
what they want/need.
> When something is bigger than you are, you do
> not argue with it. When man found all the other
> animals bigger than he was, he figured out how
> to be collectively bigger than they were.

These are obvious statements and bore me,
but power is obvious too,
and while the subject is not my favorite one, it is still one
on which I must discourse.
I choose to talk about owls, hawks & eagles,
because I really do not want to talk about men and women,
because I am tired of living with war,
because I am tired of struggling to keep my head free,
because I cannot stand to see the way humans treat each other,
because I am frightened of men who cannot control their lives
but who want to control mine,
because I am tired of receiving poison pen letters from a woman
who would like to rule my life,
because I am tired of being envied for a mythical power &
  freedom
others think I have,
because, simply because I have never tried to control anyone's life
and have often let others use me or push me around,

and I do want to talk about the birds,
rather than men,
because they are both innocent of conscience
& beyond redemption because of that innocence.
I want to talk about how much easier
my life would be
if I were the sun
and not the moon,
if I were a man, not a woman,
if I had no feelings, only desire,
if I were mercenary rather than compassionate,
if I were a gameplayer, not a humanist,
if I could stop loving you, whom I address these remarks to,
if I were an owl, or hawk, or eagle,
and my only voice were a harsh commanding cry
uttered when I killed some soft, fast-moving bloody animal
for a satisfactory meal.

But it is sunset, two days before a solar eclipse,
and summer,
in a warm place,
where I am alone,
especially alone—not even speaking the language of this country,
and I am thinking of you,
who are the sun,
tho your eyes are cold and remind me sometimes
of a snake,
though it just occurred to me
that they are sharp,
the eyes of a hunter or sportsman,
perhaps like those of a hawk or owl or eagle,
and for the first time in my life I am interested
in the idea of power,
if, in fact,
there could be a way to make you love me,
think of me,
care for me as I am fascinated by you.
But my mind wanders and is hungry for poetry,

hungry for an owl,
perhaps a barn owl, with its funny monkey face to look out of,
the infinite metaphor in its simplicity,
or for something I cannot describe,
something I call love,
yet love makes me restless,
reminds me of its terror as well as its joy.

What I want is life beyond imagination,
one that is its own
symbol, image and magic,
one that is music in a deaf world,
and I not a bird,
but for a change,
human . . .

There are those who do not believe
they can live their own lives without controlling others,
who fear that they might be dominated and ruled,
that tyranny might compel them to be sparrows rather than
   hawks,
but believe that if they ruled
the order of the world would improve.
But only with my mouth
am I a hawk,
a sharp powerful beak twists vowels into a bloody meal
every day while my hands are gentle, soft, cannot
hurt even when they are unjustly squeezed.
Oh, where do metaphors take us,
                              not beyond description?
Do they allow us to say everything but what we feel,
do they twist our ideas and make them bigger than they are?
And the meal of language, pure food,
what strength does it give us,
dieters,
imbibers of rich edibles.

Power.

Men have power over women.
A simple fact.
One I have never come to terms with.

Power.
To have your face on the cover of *Time*.
To be in *Life*.
To be rich. To be loved.
Power.

Women have the power of seduction.
Therefore all our dreams of power are dreams of love.
My life has been spent looking desperately
for love.
My fantasies are of love.
I have a monolithic view of life — all of it based around
love.

FANTASIES OF POWER

Eloping With Bobby Fischer

Dear Bobby,
   I didnt come to Reykjavik this summer,
  because that climate is like
       a wound caused by a rusty nail,
       riding a motorcycle with bare legs,
       sleeping with a man I love who refuses to touch me,
       sitting, waiting, in a duck blind during pouring rain,
  and besides
I didnt want to distract your attention,
knowing that the World Championship was important to you
and that my presence could distract you,
as the fox turns frantic
when he hears the black & tan coon hounds snuffing, panting &
barking on his trail.

You are not
a man to be seduced, I would think;
but hunted, yes,
as the solitary hunter and his fox or bear have a love affair
of ingenuity,
listening in the woods for each other,
seduction lost in the chase,
and yet the fascination of life and death gives all of us
killer
instincts when we are running,
either chasing or being chased.

    Alone
I could not help but think of you, retiring with me
to the bedroom
where chess games are not forgotten
but are played out between men and women.

I have always hated the
idea
that love between two people was a war or a game.
It is not,
in fact,
in the good life,
but who of us
lives
the good life?
And this letter is my declaration
of battle with you
or at least the hunt,
a game of sport,
Bobby,
you are a challenge to all of us women
                                can we prove
that sex
is more interesting than chess? You have ignored
us
too long,

and we are out to get you.
Right now. I'm telling you, Bobby,
that you will not be the only man in my life
until you yourself take a little interest in this game
for surely you know
that while I will exercise all my craft in hunting you
until you turn and pursue me
you will not win me, as a trophy.
Yes,
there is another World Championship up
for grabs,
the man who wins my undivided attention will be rare
and probably will have to resort to dramatic gestures
& psychological strategies.
Few have thot it a worthy tournament,
the arena of their affection being too tiny or trivial
for concentrated efforts
and I would not promote myself to any importance
either.
But game is game,
whether chess or flesh.
I could not seduce you
would pursue you instead.

Here are your competitors, Bobby,
the men I love:

First there is the King of Spain.
He has a gold tooth.
His footprints are often on the beach just at low tide
when I walk.
No one knows who my King of Spain is. I meet
him
wherever I travel,
usually near dawn,
seldom in bad weather,
he has studied the hermetic arts
and I have broken his pale narrow hand every time

he has tried to steal my heart.
He is descended from a noble family. Hunts only
with bow & arrow.

Then there is the motorcyclist & woodsman,
my betrayer,
the man who is dead & buried
but haunts my games
with the mask of an ancient bear.
I see him at truck stops.
His role is to paralyze me with fear,
to make me cry; he will help
any serious competitor
win the game from me.
He is the spirit of rice, fermented, reeking with power.

And then there is the truck driver.
Driving a baby-blue semi in his disguise.
And I?
What shall I be?
The women's chess champion?
A lady mechanic?
A skydiver?
   A silent
movie star?
No, my disguise will be to myself,
 small
 comfortable
 blonde
 laughing
 posturing
 a writer of letters
 driving a station wagon to deliver my children
 to dancing school or fencing lessons
 thinking about people
 wearing a mask of scotch and soda
and so we will never get together.

Sex is everything and nothing, like food
or sleep; who of us
would live our lives for food or sleep or sex? And yet
we die
if they are missing.
I'm hungry and sleepy and horny now.
Remember I do not believe
I should have to fight for any of these things,
am sitting alone in a world whose walls are lined with books
alone in a galaxy full of exploding suns & dis-
integrating moons
alone in a sky where I've killed off an astronomer,
once one of your rivals, Bobby,
a solar physicist who read the newspaper
when we were in bed
and who quoted newsclippings for words of love,
a man who couldnt find
the north star,
Pole, polar star,
me with my Polish anger and revolutionary etudes in my blood.
A photographer
he caught me in yellow which I wore to honor
his province, the sun,
but I was a blurred negative in his camera,
just one of the planets or asteroids
which made a good picture.
No, Bobby, there's no competition there,
even tho I'm so lonely for a steady monogamous man
I could die.

And then there is the dean of narcissistic studies,
dean of men & women,
handsome with a red mustache & green freckled eyes,
his slim hips I would accept any night in the dark.
A man whose tongue I would cut out since it articulates
a weak voice,
a voice covered with baby powder,
expressing talcum views, smug insistence

and boring needs, oh
are there any boring human needs?
They are all ticks biting into our lives & burying
their pinchered suckers
into our damp skins,
dean, dean, dean,
not Jimmy Dean,
driving your Porsche into upstate New York nights
wearing a gold seal ring
on your little finger,
decaying into a moldy version of somebody else's past & future,
unlike the woodsman & astronomer,
you were really dead before I met you;
I did not even have a chance to kill you,
our love affair was practically necrophilia,
dead dean, dead dean,
dead man.

Then
there are the letter writers, Bobby,
the young men who are married
or love other women,
who all have mustaches
and want to write more than to fuck,
and I their perfect correspondent, the vivid
letter writer who's accepted
the pen instead of the sword or cock,
writing her letters to men she can dream of,
leaving a pale empty bed each morning
with one body's imprint,
since dreamlovers dont leave wrinkled or stained sheets.
At most
a crumpled letter folded under the pillow.

Where are the men,
Bobby,
who are not homosexuals or narcissists
or playboys who make me think sex is trivial and dumb,

like fat women who make me want to swear off eating
for a year.
Where are the men
who come to the dinner table with women at night
rather than once a week in typed letters,
the fathers who stay home rather than sail the seas,
the brothers who love us without killing
themselves in remorse.
Are they all cold silent George Washingtons
or angry frustrated Beethovens,
astronomers only interested in stars,
deans, dead and invented, behind handsome mustaches,
truck drivers
who drive away,
motorcyclists betraying us small un-easy riders,
homosexual cowboys sleeping with their horses & fighting in bars,
chessmasters
who sleep with their queens before they are mated
and checked
and then never sleep at all
in the quest for the game.

Bobby, you see,
I dont even want to seduce you any more.
How could I want something so impossible.
I hate myself for these needs
and my own loneliness and anger at a world
I lament.
All the good men
are already-married men
and I envy the wives of close husbands until I realize
they think I'm a fool,
and that they envy my freedom
and the excitement of the hunt.
What can I say?
that we are all powerless,
all helpless and in pain,
all looking for love in an impossible shape

for me, the sun blazing over water,
for others, the cool moon, like an opal, egg-sized,
   in the palm,
for some, a star which is distant & slightly mysterious,
and others,
            the rings of Saturn turn dazzlingly
            like wedding bands of meteor stone,
and for all of us, the hope of life,
beyond ourselves,
the power
to breathe life into an image,
which only appears now on a sophisticated screen.

THE PARABLE OF POWER

Let me return from men to birds,
I have no power over them either.
Stories are all I have the power to tell.

Once there was a family of ospreys. There were 2 beautiful daughters in the family whom all the neighboring birds admired and many of the men were in love with. One of the young osprey beauties was a terrible flirt, while the other was quite modest and innocent of anything but her love for playing the piano. Now, despite the fact that Skinnerians have taught pigeons to play the xylophone in order to prove that behavior is learned, the beautiful young osprey who played the piano was naturally gifted and unique among her family and friends, none of whom knew much about music. (Other than singing, of course, tho the larger birds can scarcely be thought to have songs and their voices are harsh and very loud.) She loved nothing so much as the hour each day when a piano mysteriously appeared on a cliff over the sea and remained there for her talented renderings. Bach, Chopin, Beethoven, Scarlatti, Brahms—all the classics bubbled forth when she attended the instrument. But her sister who was flirtatious and only concerned with how many men admired her, discovered that if she stood near the piano while her sister was playing, many male birds, attracted by the melodious sounds would fly down and perch nearby and that she could flirt with even more coyness and charm while her sister played a Mozart sonata or a Debussy impression. The male birds, hearing the beautiful music and seeing the lovely young osprey preening herself, would forget everything but their feelings of love and desire. And, at one time or another, during the daily playing of the piano, they all proposed marriage to the beautiful and flirtatious osprey sister.

However, one irony occurred. And that is that no osprey males ever came by for these happy hours and, actually, the flirtatious young lady osprey was only interested in marriage with one of her own kind. So she always shook her beautiful head and whispered no, in such a way however as to keep the male bird wondering how he might get her to say yes the next day. One bird, a horned grebe, came every day and watched the osprey playing the piano. He scarcely noticed her sister, the flirt. And of course the horned grebe fell in love with this strange osprey sister who could play the piano.

This scene occurred every day, with a tension that increased in all the participants. It was as if a membrane, like desire, was stretched over the whole scene and each day was pulled tighter until now, our story reaches its climax—something *has* to happen. And it does. One afternoon, the piano does not appear. The osprey sister, beautiful, desperately waiting for her piano, the source of all pleasure and power for her, waits quietly, her nature being modest and undemanding. But, tho she is patient, nothing happens. For once, the piano does not appear. This is an exciting time for her sister, the flirt. Exciting because she is talking to all the birds who've gathered around and for the first time she sees among the crowd a young male osprey. He is handsome and quiet, with a large mustache, and it is obvious that he must drink bourbon, drive a sportscar, and hang out at one of the hippest bars in New York City. She is, at last, ready to fall in love. Ruffles her feathers, talks with animation to all her friends, is feeling the membrane of the day and its cumulative reality stretched tight over her body, tense with sexual possibilities.

Meanwhile, the horned grebe has gone over to speak to the piano-playing osprey sister whose piano was not appeared. She is sad but not yet in tears. She had never anticipated the possibility of the piano's not appearing, but now she understands this reality, knows it may never appear again, that in fact her whole life as she has conceived it may be over. This does not make her cry because it is too complete and intense a realization to allow anything but gradual rcognition—a piecing together of feelings that tomorrow will become sadness or pain, which will cause sorrow, tears, shock, desperation. What the horned grebe says to the piano-playing osprey is not heard by her, because just as he starts to speak, a bald eagle comes and asks if this is the group which is looking for the piano. When no one answers (as they are all afraid of the big bird) he asks his question again,

"Is this the group waiting for the piano?"

"Yes," says the horned grebe.

"Yes," says the flirtatious osprey sister (hoping the young male osprey hipster will notice her).

"Well," says the bald eagle, "I think your piano has fallen into the ocean and is about 200 feet under water."

The reactions of all the birds to this stunning announcement were just about the same. Some flew off; others started to wander away; and the two young lady ospreys sat down to think about this development in their lives. It seemed that if the piano appeared magically each day, and disappeared just as magically, nothing surely could affect such magic. That if in fact the piano fell into the sea, surely it could magically rise out of the sea again. They did not know why these things happened, who controlled them, or what had started the appearance of the piano in the first place. However, they decided that whatever Power this might be, was the Power they must seek and appeal to, so that the young lady osprey's piano would come back. The male osprey was standing talking to the horned grebe in low tones, and they turned to the two beautiful ospreys and offered this plan for retrieving the piano. The osprey and the grebe knew of a large fishnet used by a group of local fishermen, and they thought they might gather about 100 birds together and go out and use the net to pull the piano up out of the ocean. The bald eagle thought that was possible too, so the men went off to gather up their cronies and to embark on the rescue mission.

However, the osprey sisters were conferring about the nature of the magic which must control the piano and which consequently was the only thing they felt could restore it. They remembered that the first time the piano had appeared there had been a full moon and they had been sitting in the trees watching it. They had wished something would happen to make their lives more exciting and not more than an hour later, the shape of the piano had shone in silhouette against the moon, and the next day the one osprey sister was practicing her scales. They decided the moon was perhaps responsible for the piano and decided to write her a letter requesting the return of the piano. This is the letter they wrote:

Dear Moon,
We loved your piano and are sad without it. May we know why you have taken it away? And if there is any way we can get it back?
Sincerely,
The Osprey Sisters

They put it in the mailbox and went to sleep.

In the meantime the male birds were assembling near the fishermen's net and getting ready to try to haul the piano up out of the sea. It was, indeed, as the bald eagle had said, 200 feet under water. When about 100 birds were assembled, they picked the net up in their beaks and flew with it to the spot where the piano was submerged. The diving birds then took corners of the net and dove under water with it, wrapping it around the piano, tho with difficulty as the piano was wedged into a deep sand bar and they had to keep diving down to dig parts of it out so that the net would fit underneath. They could see the job would take more than a day, so when the net was partially secured, in fatigue they all went to sleep for a few hours.

The next day, when the mail arrived, there was a letter addressed to the osprey sisters and the return address in the corner bore the imprint of the moon—a pale white stain, crescent shaped. The letter said:

Dear Osprey Sisters,
Only the men who love you have the power to restore your piano. There is nothing I can do.
With regrets,
The Moon

The osprey sisters knew there were men who loved and cared about them, but they did not really think any of them had the strength to pull the piano out of the ocean. However, they went over to the place where all the action was, for the male birds were awake again and trying to complete the difficult task.

Now, those of you who read fables and parables know that I must have figured out some possible ending for this story, either to prove that love is all-powerful or to prove that it's not. Any of you readers who are used to Wakoski's stories are more likely to think that I will give a long, meditative, not-very-story-like ending to the tale, which will turn out to be a discussion of ethics or morality. But I would like to surprise all the readers by ending this story in quite another way entirely. What if I invent a rowboat full of angry fishermen who come rowing up with the giant moon, like a great blow-fish, lying in the boat, breathing heavily like the belly of a caught fish, with gills hopelessly opening and closing, out of breath from having been chased through the sky by the fishermen and now hurt, bleeding scarlet drops against the pale face, and the fishermen dumping her into the ocean, ordering her to retrieve the big net so necessary to their occupation, and the moon bobbing and protesting she can do nothing, till she sinks into the water and lies sadly at the bottom of the sea. The birds have been frightened away. The osprey sisters cry on the shore. The fishermen cannot get back their net which is tangled impossibly around the grand piano. The birds have no language and fly off singly, wondering how they had believed in such an unreal scene. The fishermen cannot retrieve the moon either, because power is easily lost simply trying to exercise it. We now live in a dark world where we only imagine a moon, where love is irrelevant, and life projects are as easily scattered as a flock of birds. Concepts are random, risky as chaos. We hold the world together for small moments which add up to an hour of piano playing each day, flirtation while there's music, writing letters to the moon.

GREED, Part 12

The Greed To Be Fulfilled

And flowers, to my thinking, are not merely pretty-pretty. They have in their fragrance an earthiness of the humis and the corruptive earth from which they spring. And pansies, in their streaked faces, have a look of many things besides heartsease.
. . .
A flower passes, and that perhaps is the best of it. If we can take it in its transience, its breath, its maybe mephistophelian, maybe paley ophelian face, the look it gives, the gesture of its full bloom, and the way it turns upon us to depart — that was the flower, we have had it, and no immortelle can give us anything in comparison.
. . . don't nail the pansy down. You won't keep it any better if you do.

> D.H. Lawrence, from the foreword
> to *Pansies,* 1929

There are about 200,000 known types of flowers with at least 32,000 of them being classified as wild flowers.

Wild flowers grow almost everywhere and they require no attention. You'll find them blooming in woods, deserts, jungles, fields, meadows and swamps.

Woodland wild flowers thrive on deep, rich humus, fleshy decaying leaves and wood. Many bloom in early spring when the most sun hits the forest floor, but others bloom later on and do well with only the small amount of sunlight that filters through the leaves of overhanging trees.

Desert wild flowers probably have the most unfavorable conditions of all plants. Rain usually falls only during a very brief season, and the rest of the year sun usually bakes the sandy soil.

> from "Ask Andy" column,
> May 13, 1981
> *Atlanta Constitution*

There is a music slings itself toward me.
Not frog. If only it were frog. The awful strum,
followed by clicking castenets
no lilypad orchestra could summon up,
night in the land of the Frog Prince or Gunslinger, where
  American
women go,
fat night of denial,
night of imperfect bodies,
the voices, a chorus furious with bees.
John Cage, La Monte Young, stand up, take a bow.
You are creating a world
where music obeys us, instead of we
obeying it.
Can we ever make the body go
where the mind goes?

Night where we dream of being invisible.
Ellen West, an aberration of what we all,
since Emerson, have sought:
disembodiment.
                Oh, M., you especially,
and I, Diane,
the Body,
so substantial not one can deny it. Oh, M.,
you were wrong, not even my lips are thin,
from them come the fat frog words of
green summer (my garden, a man's body,
the tomatoes hanging on the vines, full sacks of seed,
the firm cucumbers inching their way
into (erection), the beans hidden among
heart-shaped leaves,
the purple grapes beyond in the vineyard
gathering a bloom that includes both the
acid and sweet of Homer, Milton, old clarets,
the *nouveau beaujolais* of Frank O'Hara,
and the beginning of a big big burgundy, Charles Olson.

A long black car, an Oldsmobile, polished
like Baccarat, calls for me,
driven by that dalmatian I once thought
was you. He'll take me
the regular route,
down Morning Street, down Evening Street,
and then to someplace where only masks indicate reality.
How I love this long drive, locked in the air conditioned car,
one rose in a Lalique car-vase against the back of the driver's
seat. I'll change it each day of the journey, taking a
representative flower wherever I am.
Already,
I give up the rose
for one graceful feathered crown of Wild Bergamot.
This is Michigan
I'm starting from.

There is a poetry beyond pain.
It comes with the anaesthesia of aging.
There is a moment where the greatest satiation comes through
the eye. Only
alone can anyone know this.
Only without the worldly sense of known and needed. The point
where the body feeds on itself.

We were riding through the desert
though the air conditioned car kept us,
the driver and me,
                cool
and untouched. The other voice who wants to   STRUM
keeps a cadence moving
in my head. Should I part the curtain
STRUM (pause)
STRUM (pause)
Go away, I tell this voice which once
was smaller than I, and now owns the whole desert.

"We are driving to Wood Butcher Ranch,

owned by the poet, Norman Hindley," I say
to the driver, but by now
I see my driver is far more mysterious than I previously supposed.
Not a simple dalmatian sitting behind the wheel wearing a fireman's hat,
his spotted paws guiding the gliding car over wide smooth empty
desert roads. He turns down a winding drive, off the highway,
the car bumping along as the track narrows, becomes only a rut,
and we finally stop at a spot where it seems as if there is nothing
but the beginning of low foothills. There are saguaro cacti
taller than oaks and in one of them, an owl, the size of an alarm
clock, sticks his head and whole body from a hollow in one
arm of the cactus. We get out and walk. The day is cooling toward dusk. I don't know why we've stopped or where we are going. I know only the elegant dalmatian who walks on two paws
and now appears to be wearing elaborately patterned Tony Lamas
boots with giant roses on them, possesses a kind of silence which
commands me and which I cannot refuse. I follow him up the
crest, winding through rocks which make me very nervous,
knowing there must be rattlers, and we soon stop. At this point,
I am suddenly aware of a most remarkable sight. Ahead there is a
plateau and on it, the most stunning building I have ever seen. It
almost seems invisible. made completely out of many-faceted glass.
Seemingly, a three-storied building transparent and composed of
cubes, angles and points. At times it seems to disappear, at other
times it sparkles like a mountain of diamonds. Though it appears
transparent I can see nothing in it. In fact, perhaps it is only a
construction, a sculpture, an empty geometric puzzle. Even a
mirage. The dalmatian and I start walking again, and I realize that
the glass building is perhaps half a mile away. When we reach the
building we find a dazzling crystal arch over which is the legend
> BLOOD FACTORY

I now saw that the glass structure was a huge wall surrounding,
what? I walked through the arch which must have been at least
twenty feet tall and found myself not in the desert but in a garden, an abundant garden, and another crystal structure which I
took to be a kind of castle was snuggled in there. Or were there

many? The dalmatian had disappeared by this time and the sun glittered and glinted, desert scorching, except that ahead appeared this what? mirage? the glass illusion?

Perhaps I should mention, at this point, the silence. An attribute of the desert, of my life at this time and of this place I was now standing. Utter and complete silence. I felt clear too. As if I could sing and my voice would produce the purest *bel canto*.

Since the dalmatian had disappeared, I decided to explore timidly the garden. For its very abundance and lushness seemed the most unbelievable part of this whole vision. The desert is a place which allows one to expect the illusion of a shimmering building, even a crystal city, but to find this structure surrounded by a garden somehow did surprise me. The oasis is a kind of intrinsic mirage, for no one expects green, the shade of trees (even palms) or cool water or any kind of glade after the miles and miles of sand, of barren landscape.

So, I walked along a path with tall japonica bushes on one side, the leaves waxy and burnished, the flowers with their pure white and pink perfect petals seeming to be cut from jade or quartz. On the other side were hundreds of rose bushes covered with smooth fragrant buds and full flowers with petals that drew bees whose buzz began to give the day a rich hum. The blazing transparent structure still seemed close but as I walked it did not seem to come closer, and while this interested me, it did not trouble me. Measuring or judging distances has always been a weak point of my vision. I was used to things seeming closer or especially farther away than they actually were.

I came to a clearing which in another setting might have been a lawn. But here I was reminded that we were in the desert. There was nothing but sand and one clump of tall palm trees. Under the trees, there was a huge oriental carpet, a Kazak, its geometric shapes glowing against the sand, and on it in a huge leather chair sat a man holding a large orange cat in his lap. He, too,

was huge. With my terrible sense of perspective, I knew I could
be wrong in my estimations of his size, but I thought he must be
at least six foot four and somewhat stout.

There was a parting in the rosebush hedge which allowed me to
leave the path and walk toward the cluster of palms. But as I
passed through the hedge I noticed a small sign near the ground,
as if it were a botanical tag or notice, saying,
        SOCIETY FOR WESTERN FLOWERS
             G. WASHINGTON, Pres.
I started to walk across the sand over to the palm-shaded, carpeted
glade but suddenly noticed to my left a large dark coil, like a
pile of rope, lying on the sand and realized to my horror
that it was a rattlesnake. At once I was frozen. I couldn't
move. My whole interior was lurching and racing,
but my body itself was paralyzed. What should
I do? I heard a voice somewhat high and cracked. It was the
man in the chair on the rug, undoubtedly G. Washington, Pres.,
and he was saying, "One foot in front of the other. One foot
in front of the other. Mother is sleepy today. Bring your letters
and diamonds to me. The Society is waiting for your news."

I was beginning to feel like Alice, but decided to enjoy it rather
than fight. I pretended I was a gladiola and put one foot in
front of another, until I left the snake far behind and finally
stood on the rug near G. Washington.

The rug I was standing on was an early Cloudbound Kazak, the
reds glowing with an orange hue and two large green medallions
with s-shaped patterns the colour of sand. I was arrested by the
fact that on the crab borders of linked rosettes there were actually
sitting a row of what looked like crab shells and, as I stood
there one of them seemed to move. Having gotten past the rattler
I didn't really want an encounter with any other form of wildlife.
But what do you expect (I suppose) if you embark on a journey
with a dalmatian as a driver.

G. Washington, Pres., was an enormous man. I had always felt in the past that my George Washington should be placed in the West, given a life in a hot country, that so much of his history was corrupted and repressed with geographic strictures. After all, as a young man he had become a surveyor precisely because he needed new territory and land of his own; and it has always been my feeling that some old American passenger-pigeon instinct in him pointed him West. He just never got far enough West in the 18th century.

So, now, here he was, 200 years later; sitting in a leather chair on an ancient Caucasian carpet in the Western desert, having mysteriously become the head of an organization known as The Society For Western Flowers. In front of him was a table made of a huge redwood burl, holding a calico teapot, two cups and a heavy Steuben vase containing one bird-of-paradise flower.

"Mr. President," I said timidly.
"The girl who is looking for The King of Spain, I presume?" he said. "I have always felt you wanted to be The Queen of Spain and The First Lady. Is that true?"

They *were* crabs lining up on the border of the rug. I knew for sure now, as one the size of my hand started sideling over to the table, or maybe it was toward my foot. I was beginning to be nervous again, and I really had no answer to his questions. That is, there was so much I had been wanting to say to this man over the years and yet, each year, I realized more that I didn't really know if I could ultimately say anything.

"Will you have tea?" said The President.
"Yes," I nodded.
And he poured me a cup of one of my favorite strong black Assam teas, probably from Fortnum and Mason.

"Richard Brautigan once had tea with Emily Dickinson," I said. "But this is better, I think. Having tea with George Washington."

He was silent. It was cool under the palm trees and suddenly I felt very much at peace, at ease on the brilliant Caucasian rug, drinking my tea and being in the presence of The President of The Society for Western Flowers.

And as I was sitting there, so much at ease, enjoying myself with the comfort of beautiful objects, I realized that this was gluttony. The essence of greedy consumption; this desire for peace, for satiation, for satisfaction and fulfillment; *this*, not some orgy of ridiculous display, was the real gluttonous greed of our culture. To have enough. And a bit more. To never be wanting. To possess and enjoy each thing desired, to always be filled, to have the feeling of filling and being filled with objects, foods, feelings, situations that one wanted. To want but then never to be wanting.

It struck me that the only fact which had saved me from suffering all my life from this American norm of gluttony, bourgeois fulfillment or satisfaction, was my childhood and young adulthood of poverty and my ignorance of how to make a middle-class life for myself. But that, now, I too was just another gluttonous insensitive bourgeois sitting and drinking tea with The President.

He broke my reverie by saying, "You think you have made your longest journey here to this spot. But your real journey is ahead of you. I know what your thoughts are and they have just begun to prepare you for the real journey. You are going to change the nature of your quest. Tell me, what do you think you have searched for all these years?"

"The perfect man, I suppose."
"Or?"
"Or, the perfect match or mate, I guess."
"Or?"
"A feeling of completion, fulfillment."
"Have you found that?"
"Well, yes, in a way. Just sitting here in the sun, in this

Western garden, on your magnificent rug, drinking good black tea from a delicate cup, and talking to you, my important father, makes me feel that way. Complete. Fulfilled. And I feel that way when I am tending my plants or growing new plants. I feel that way when I cook in my well-equipped kitchen or sleep in my bed with extravagant sheets and soft comforters and many pillows tucked around me. I feel that drinking a good glass of wine, listening to classical music or reading a book. And I feel that way with the man from receiving at Sears (ironically, I met him in Spain)."
"So your quest is over?"
I felt stupid because I knew he was Socrates and I the slave and that he was leading me to an idea that had been nudging me, but one I didn't really know how to approach. Not a religious or spiritual idea, but one of almost appalling crassness.
"Yes, my quest is over."
"Then why are you here?"
"To begin my journey," I said the words almost as if I had been drugged and they were a script I was reciting from brainwashed memory.

"Who am I?" he said.
Again, as if I were a robot, "You are The President of The Society for Western Flowers."
"Here is a mask," he said and gave me what looked like a large gorgeous pansy made of purple and yellow and brown silk with holes for my eyes and mouth. It tied over my face. "Now, you are my secretary," he said. "And you may stay here for the performance."
I was a little disappointed. "Why do I always have to be somebody's secretary? Couldn't I have some other title?"

"All right," he said, "You are now *Pensées*." Soon, while I was sitting there, I heard a rustling sound and saw that about thirty people had joined us, each wearing the mask of a flower. There were roses, of course, and sunflowers, a variety of orchids, some iris, poppies, ranunculi and chicory. There were both men and women under the masks, some of which slipped over the entire head, unlike mine, so that I could not even see the hair, while others tied over the face as mine did. I looked to see if there were any other pansies. There was one. I thought the mask was worn by a boy, but could not be sure.

All this time, G. Washington was sitting in his chair with the orange cat in his lap. He drank a cup of tea and then simply sat there while the masked people came into the garden and arranged themselves on and around the carpet. After everyone seemed to be settled, he took the bird-of-paradise out of its vase and shook it. Some petals struck against the table making a small chiming sound. "Will the meeting of The Society for Western Flowers please come to order," said The President. "Our guest, Diane, has finally arrived after a most interesting journey. But I have persuaded her that her real journey is still ahead of her. First we will perform the masque, then we will have the award ceremony and finally we will have the questioning. During the entire meeting, we will enjoy the banquet."

I had been absorbed first in watching the president, then in observing the masked guests as they came in and arranged themselves and finally moved my attention back to The President as he opened this meeting, so that I was completely unaware of when and how our setting had changed. Not drastically, but slowly I began to realize that the carpet had been growing larger and larger. Surely, it would have taken a century of knot-tying to produce a magnificent rug of these huge dimensions. And now there seemed to be tables and chairs scattered around it while behind The President a huge buffet loaded with food had appeared. Somehow, at once we knew that we should find our places around these small tables, and when we sat down, I found myself at a table with an iris and a paphiopedilum. They both seemed to be women. I looked for the other pansy and saw him somewhere on the other side of the rug. Our table was close to The President's chair and in the shade of the original clump of palms. On our table were three wine glasses. A pair of white gloved hands hovered over the table and a voice above them asked if we would like sangria. We all said yes.

A pitcher full of dark burgundy-coloured liquid with slices of orange floating in it appeared in the gloves and poured the goblets full of punch. I asked for an ice cube or two and was immediately served three ice cubes from silver tongs by another pair of gloved hands which had not been there a moment before.

Night on the desert is for those of us who have been city dwellers like being in another plane or dimension. The clarity of the air, the brilliance of the stars, the contrasting blackness of the sky, and each object, including one's self, seeming to be discrete, intense and unusual. Perhaps it is this very sense that people search for when immersing themselves in dream and drug worlds. Yet, in the instance of this occasion, the ceremony itself seemed to be a reflection of the landscape and an organic extension of the desert night.

To have 30 people disguised or masked as flowers is surely a bit absurd, but what more appropriate costume for The Society for Western Flowers meeting? I felt that it was natural that I had been given a pansy mask, since that had been my favorite flower as a child, and then when I discovered that D.H. Lawrence, one of my favorite writers, had entitled his collections of poems, *Pansies,* of course punning on the french word *pensées* I had felt even more connection with that flower. All of my life I have hated the denigrating image of women as flowers, as a kind of implication of weakness, lack of profundity or depth. Women's clubs and gardening clubs being almost synonymous with frivolity, the implication that women have nothing better to do with their time than grow and pick and arrange flowers, a decorative and non-functional reality. So, it pleased me to see George Washington, The Father of Our Country, here in the improbable desert with his impossible garden, presiding over the Flower Society and, in fact, presenting its members as human flowers.

A script was passed out by the white gloved hands to all of us, and The President rose and began to speak, "This evening's masque will be performed from this script. Each one of you will know what part you are to play as soon as I call the name of the character. Or you should know. This masque was written by Diane, though she will claim that she has never seen the script before."

It was true. I certainly had never written a play, a masque or even a dramatic poem in my lifetime. And while I savoured the title, "Looking For The King of Spain," it seemed as if The President might not be taking me too seriously. That is, if I was really here to identify a new quest, a new journey, why was it going to be introduced with an old title, the title of an old quest?

"I will now introduce the characters of our play." The President was speaking again. "Step forward, The King of Spain." A tall, slender man wearing the face mask of a brilliant red opium poppy stood up. He had been sitting at a table with a beautiful woman with long black hair wearing the mask of a magnolia blossom. He looked rather effete to me, and I thought somewhat resentfully that this was not actually my concept of The King of Spain. However when he smiled he did flash a gold tooth and I thought, "Oh well, this is a play. It's all costumes and talk. What does it matter?"

The President was speaking again. "The second character in our masque tonight is George Washington." Since *he* was George Washington, I didn't know what this portly old gentleman was going to do. He wasn't wearing a flower mask himself, and he seemed to enjoy being master of ceremonies. But I didn't even have a chance to start speculating before a big bearlike man with shoulders designed for wrestling (Gorgeous George) rose and bowed. He had shoulder-length greying hair which was tied into a pony-tail and was wearing a down vest over his workshirt and jeans. He wore logger's boots and a leather hat with a fairly wide brim. Round wire-rimmed glasses. He was holding his mask in his hand, rather sheepishly, as if the large sunflower were a small daisy and not really what he should be holding. I expected to see a carpenter's kit and wood shavings at his feet, but actually he was simply sitting at a table with four young girls all wearing the masks of sweet peas over their heads and from their bodies looking as if they might not be more than 13 or 14 years old. This was George Washington? I couldn't tell if The President of The Western Flower Society was smiling or not. A little like the Mona Lisa, that ambiguous tight-stretched mouth always seemed to be on the verge of some expression, but one was never quite sure of what. Surely he found his namesake for the play rather sardonic? Well, by now I knew fairly certainly that our Pres., G.W., had probably written this play and was palming it off on me. But the whole event was not really one I could question. I still felt more excitement and anticipation than anything else. It didn't really matter if I was misunderstood tonight. What was happening simply took precedence over understanding.

"And the third character in our play will be Beethoven." With this announcement, three different men stood up. One of them had been sitting at a table with three other men wearing the masks of daffodils. The table was surrounded by electronic equipment and instrument cases including a large set of drums. I had guessed that they were a rock band, though I really felt that some other type of music would be more appropriate for a masque performed on the desert by a cast of characters invented by Diane Wakoski. Still, I had to remind myself that G.W. had probably written this masque and these characters from my poems were only an illusion or something to hook me into an unusual event. The second man who stood up was sitting at a table alone. He, like the first Beethoven, was short and slender with shoulder length curly hair and long thin hands which stuck out quite a bit from the cuffs of his jacket. Oddly, they looked a little like twins, both wearing maroon brocaded coats and very tight velvet pants and, frankly, to my bourgeois eye, looking like they mainlined heroin or some amphetamine; in other words, unhealthy and with crazy artificial energy. The third man who stood up, in contrast, was extremely fat, though not terribly tall either. Perhaps about 5'10' or so, and he wore a long burnous-style robe, very short hair and, of all things, a monocle. His very fat hands seemed to be conducting some silent piece of music, and he smiled and beamed at everyone around him. He was sitting at a table with two very beautiful blond boys who had laid their rose masks on the table beside them. Oh brother, I thought, this is about as far away from my concept of Beethoven as you can get. I also despaired at what kind of music this fat pseudo-monk would make, and it then occurred to me to wonder about the second Beethoven who looked so much like the first, but who was sitting alone and seemingly not part of the rock group. What was his music like, for heaven's sake? I was never to find out.

"The fourth character," said our President, "The Blue Moon Cowboy." A blond man entirely dressed in baby blue studded with rhinestones stood up. His Western shirt, with snap buttons, was perfectly tailored to fit his thin body, his baby-blue denim jeans were so tight that he almost seemed to have a codpiece. His Stetson was baby blue and his boots had stiletto toes outlined in silver but they were blue too. Another $800 Tony Lamas creation, I supposed. I wonder where these cowboys get their cash. But of course I knew: Hollywood. I expected him to start crooning, "Blue moon/ I saw you standing alone/ Without a care in the world/ Without a love of my own," but thank God the Pres. didn't give him a chance. Commercial cowboys? Is that what people thought I meant? This really was getting to be an exercise in misunderstanding. But either the sangria was making me too laid-back to care, or the desert air was giving me perspective I didn't usually have when hearing people's misinterpretations of my poems. Where in the world did that fool Judson Jerome ever get the idea that My Mother's Milkman was black? Probably the same place that Marjorie Perloff got the idea that I hung out in truck stops. What incredible prejudices people read into poems to create their misinterpretations. But the occasion seemed too strong for thinking about trivial matters.

"The fifth and sixth characters in 'Waiting For The King of Spain' will be the Woodsman and the Mechanic." One man with the mask of a violet stood up. He had an axe in one hand and a large wrench in the other. His mask was tiny and actually only fit over his nose. A shrinking violet? The effect was surreal at best, in fact quite comical. His body was heavy and broad. His hair, dark, and combed with a lot of grease in a kind of '40s pompadour. The violet mask on the end of his nose was really more like a butterfly sitting there or some oddly beautiful mole. This is definitely what you get for judging people by their looks, I thought. Boy oh boy, Diane. Is this what people see in your poems?

"The seventh character this evening will be Diane herself. Stand up, Diane." I started to rise, but saw across the room the other pansy mask rising. It was a young thin boy, I thought, but when he took off his mask, I saw an older man and I have to say that my first thought was that he was an aging queen. What is there about certain men's faces which makes you know that they are lovers of other men? I don't mean swishy mannerisms, or coy talk, or anything obvious like feminine hairstyles, etc. There is something about that androgynous face, neither man nor woman which seems to me like a mirror for pain anywhere I see it. So, this guy was going to be Diane in the masque. Oh, well. Couldn't be any worse than the way people actually misread my poems, could it? This desert air definitely made one care less. I began wondering if I shouldn't move to the desert. Especially if I were going to spend my life being misunderstood. It was so much easier here.

"And the final character in tonight's play will be a new character, one Diane has just this minute decided to introduce to her poems, The Devil." Nothing at this point could have surprised me. And actually, this seemed like rather a good idea. Old G.W. had certainly been creating a diabolical cast of characters for my masque and giving demonic interpretations to my muses. Why not The Devil himself? I hope he's given him a speaking part, I thought. I remembered that recently a young actress had told me that the most interesting role she ever understudied was that of a deaf mute. Maybe she was joking, but I took her seriously. Still, I wanted at this point for The Devil to have a speaking part. Was he the one who was going to tell me what my new journey was going to be? Or was he there to beguile me and lead me off in the wrong direction? Surely, my own characters as presented so far seemed to be going off in a fairly different direction than I myself thought I had gone. But here we all were, at The Society for Western Flowers, meeting on the desert, waiting to be entertained. What allegory, I wondered, would I, that is George, have chosen for the action of the masque?

I looked around to see who would stand up, when the Devil was announced. It was the proverbial tall, dark and handsome man who stood up, and when he took of his mask which covered his whole head, a mask in the shape of a black calla lily, I was aghast because he was M., the man I had once been married to, and whom I still occasionally had troubled dreams about. Well, here was one time when old George Washington seemed to be 100% correct. Still, since he seemed to have something up his sleeve with all the other characters, I wondered what trick of his mind this Devil was going to represent. But I had no time for introspection, as The President said, "Now, let the play begin."

As he was settling his coat around his stout body and holding his cup so that the gloves would pour him a bit of tea, the dalmatian who had driven me to this place ran up to him, barking, and as he fondled the dog he leaned down and apparently was given a message. The dog sat down at the table with The President, and The President rose again, saying, "The title of tonight's masque has been changed. It will be called, 'The Moon Loses Her Shoes.' "

Now, the four rock musicians including the first Beethoven were shown in the spotlight. They had assembled all their instruments next to The President's table, complete with microphones, and the sign on the drum said, "The Moon's Shoes." The first Beethoven had a saxophone around his neck and he looked even more disreputable than I had earlier thought. Under his brocaded coat he had no shirt and his pants looked (I hate to say it) pee-stained. He had old scuffed wingtip shoes and was wearing them with no sox. Even though this was the desert, the missing shirt and sox seemed more likely to be from indigence and a bum's life than an urge to be cool. Besides, it was actually quite chilly. A large bonfire had been built behind The President's table. And the white gloves were passing around down jackets to any of the guests/players who wanted them. I was wearing my long black Irish cape, but was getting chilly in spite of it and gratefully took a down vest to snuggle into under the cape. The rock group launched into a medley of 1960s Beach Boys tunes, I suppose because of me and my dated desires. Actually, I was pleased because I was sure that they would rather be performing some cacophonous new tunes of their own. After singing "Little Deuce Coupe" the first Beethoven said into his mike, "Good evening, Ladies and Gentlemen. We are The Moon's Shoes, coming to you from the desert meeting of The Society for Western Flowers, sponsored by G. Washington, Pres., and we want to thank you all for coming out tonight and giving us your support. During the evening we intend to be more than just the little rock group that you think you see standing in front of you. We are going to perform compositions by John Cage, La Monte Young, Terry Riley, Philip Glass, Beethoven, Mozart, and yours truly, Ludwig B. Lunar. The first number on our program will be performed simultaneously with the performance of the masque. It is a piece inspired by La Monte Young which consists of a note located between middle C and B, played on the saxophone but with a reed invented by Composer Young which allows a skilled performer to sustain the note without interruption for up to three hours. I have spent the past four weeks practicing the piece and as a result must apologize for my appearance. My shirt became so soaked with sweat that it finally fell off and my socks developed some vibration that unravelled them. I didn't dare let go of the note long enough to go shopping for new clothes. Actually, this rap must sound pretty strange to you, but I used to be into threads and know that my appearance might give my namesake, Old Ludwig B., a bad name. Say, is there anybody in the audience named Bukowski? I heard he was a pal of Ludwig's. Hi there, Buk. Want to dedicate this performance of 'The Long Note' (that's the name of the piece) to you."

I couldn't believe that Charles Bukowski, alias Hank Chinaski, one of the best poets in the world, was here tonight. But then by now, nothing should have seemed unusual to me. And there he was. A big guy with a pock-marked face and a white shirt with the sleeves rolled up past the elbows. I had heard that he was reformed from his beer-drinking and womanizing ways, and was now drinking only expensive German wine, eating health food and, in fact, living with the girl who owned the health food store. However, he had a bottle of Budweiser in his hand. Perhaps it contained Moselle? I couldn't imagine him drinking sangria, no matter how good (made with freshly squeezed orange juice). It would be just so much fruit punch to him. Kool Aid on the desert. I looked to see if he had a flower mask. God forbid. Can you imagine what Bukowski would say about flower clubs, flower masks, etc.? But there it was, around his wrist, like a corsage on a prom date—a purple cattleya. This had to be somebody's joke.

Ludwig B. Lunar put his saxophone to his mouth, a position he would not relinquish for the next two hours. I felt rather shabby about my judgmental attitude concerning his neglected appearance. He was an artist. Someone who cared more about music, his performance, his integrity, than worldly things. And here was I, always saying I didn't care about the worldly, judging him negatively because of his worldly (out of this worldly) appearance. Is it a reciprocity? The more we are misunderstood, the more we are destined to misunderstand others? Was this whole evening meant to be simply a kind of moral lesson for me, rather than an adventure, a casting of myself into a new journey or quest?

Now for the *Masque*. I am going to describe what I saw and put my descriptions in parentheses. I will simply indicate the names of the characters in conventional play format, and try to quote their lines. Oh, I have the script in front of me. But given how strange everything has been so far, who knows if they are even meant to follow it? Perhaps, if they digress or get diverted, I'll interject that information.

The Moon Loses Her Shoes
Act I

(Standing onstage are George Washington, wearing his sunflower mask, and The King of Spain, wearing his scarlet poppy. Both masks cover their faces. They make a strong contrast, these two characters. George Washington, so burly. The King of Spain, so thin. And their costumes so different from each other, one rough and masculine, the other almost effeminate.)

KING OF SPAIN: In the name of all the magic I possess, and wearing the cap of darkness, I bestow this gift on your daughter, Diane, The Moon: a pair of satin shoes, which she may wear all of her life. They will grow with her, they will never soil; they will always be fresh and white and glowing. As she walks across the sky each night of her life, the shoes will give her grace and she, in her journey, will never tire. As long as she wears these shoes, her light will enchant men and she will be adored, sometimes even worshipped. She will protect and cherish with her light, but the shoes will insure a nightly journey that never is broken. She must never allow her shoes to be removed or taken away, for then her journey will be erratic and tiring. She will not have the power to create Romance in the hearts of men or allow them to understand darkness without her shoes.

GEORGE WASHINGTON: For my daughter, Diane, The Moon, I accept this gift and promise to protect her from its loss during my lifetime. May I bring her up in wisdom so that she honors the power of these magic shoes and never is tempted, by even the Devil, to remove them or to allow them to be lost.

(Diane, wearing a long skirt and his/her pansy mask, comes on stage.)

GEORGE WASHINGTON: Here, my dear, are the magic shoes which guarantee you to be Queen of the Night. I give them to you, as your father, but they come from The King of Spain who loves you and wishes to illuminate the darkness with your soft light. Never take off these shoes, even in love. No one will ever have the power to take them off you, for with them, all men will love you and even worship you, and none would do you harm. Thus, it is your will that you must guard and your desire. You are mistress of your shoes. They will guide your life and keep the moon brilliant in the sky.

DIANE: What if some man loves me and needs my shoes to save his life?

GEORGE WASHINGTON: Your shoes will not save a man's life. But your own life will be much less without the shoes. The Moon's Shoes are her shoes, and can only bring her pure worship when she wears them.

DIANE: (somewhat petulantly) But what if I want to bathe? Surely I will be the only woman in the world who wears her shoes in the bathtub? And what if I want to wear a new style sometime? Why must I wear the same old shoes all my life? Why is that such a great gift?

GEORGE WASHINGTON: My dear, magic gifts are magic. You are supposed to be overwhelmed and love them. Put them on right now. I am sure that once these slippers are on your feet you will never want any others.

(He/she sits down on the floor and puts on the white slippers. As she does, a glow begins to surround her and there is no ambiguity about her appearance. She is all woman. Dressed in white, her pansy mask only seeming now to make shadows on her face rather than covering it, she is radiant. Everyone feels her glow and her power.)

DIANE: Father. How could I have ever questioned you? The shoes are perfect.

(From offstage, the voice of The King of Spain is heard saying:

"You will never see me, but I will follow you everywhere and remind you that the shoes will make all men love you. The influence of The Moon is the influence of poetry, of the softening of the night's black.")

(Exit GEORGE WASHINGTON and DIANE.)

(Now The Blue Moon Cowboy comes on stage and walks over to the second Beethoven.)

BLUE MOON COWBOY: Hey, Beethoven Two, I have just written this love song to The Moon, and I wonder if you would compose some music for it?

BEETHOVEN II: You know I am not avant-garde like The First Beethoven?

BLUE MOON COWBOY: That doesn't matter. In fact, I think it might be better. I know that The Moon admires new things, but that she loves old ones.

(The Devil walks onstage and turns to The Blue Moon Cowboy)

DEVIL: You're just the man I want to see. I understand that you are in love with The Moon.

BLUE MOON COWBOY: I am dedicated to The Moon. I am called The Blue Moon Cowboy because I love her so much and know that she can never love me in return. Actually, as you probably know, a cowboy's life is really not suited for women and marriage and all that. So, it's probably just as well for me. If I were married, I might not be able to afford these clothes, and they really suit me well.

DEVIL: Do you know about The Moon's Shoes?

BEETHOVEN II: Hey, man, that's the name of our group. We are The Moon's Shoes.

DEVIL: Oh, are you The Moon's Shoes? Actually, I'm referring to The Moon's actual shoes. The magic ones.

BLUE MOON COWBOY: "The Moon walks in her silver shooen." Walter de la Mare, I think. Old Romantic poetry.

DEVIL: Well, yes. But actually, did you know that The Moon is George Washington's daughter? The first president of the U.S. He became a surveyor in order to acquire some wealth, and in going West he met this beautiful Indian woman in the forest one night, and they had a child who became The Moon. Of course, George couldn't let on about this back home, because he was married to Martha, and running for President and all, but like all old lechers he loves the illegitimate daughter best. So, he made a deal with The King of Spain who was looking around out West also and hoping to acquire some land, and The King of Spain, who is invisible, agreed to be the godfather to this daughter, Moon. As his christening gift, he gave her these magic shoes which she wears all the time. They are what make all men love and worship the moon. What if you had the shoes, Blue Moon? After all, your name sort of entitles you to them. You could go on the circuit and become as successful as Conway Twitty or Wayne Newton or Willie Nelson.

(The Blue Moon Cowboy looks thoughtful.)

BLUE MOON COWBOY: But I love the moon. I wouldn't want to steal her shoes.

DEVIL: Look at it this way. The Moon will never love you. But she is rather soft-hearted. Maybe, if you plead with her, she will give you the shoes.

BLUE MOON COWBOY: But why would she give her magic shoes away? You must be out of your mind, Devil. She couldn't give them to me, or to anybody.

DEVIL: Maybe. But isn't it worth a try?

(Enter the third Beethoven in his monk's robe.)

DEVIL: Hello, Big B.

3RD BEETHOVEN: Well, well, well, Devil. What are you doing here? Stirring up a little trouble? I haven't seen you since that Gay Rights parade last year. What *are* you doing here?

DEVIL: Always looking for idle hands. No, actually, I was giving some good advice to the Cowboy here. He's in love with The Moon, and I suggested that he ask The Moon to give him her shoes.

3RD BEETHOVEN: Why in heaven would The Moon give away her magic shoes, Devil? Are you suggesting that the Cowboy's poetry is so beautiful it can charm the shoes off The Moon?

DEVIL: Well, it might be.

BLUE MOON COWBOY: I am honored that you like my poetry so well. I guess I'd better go and work on my ode to The Moon. You're right. It's worth a try. You know, I believe in trying. I enter everything. The Yale Younger Poets. Apply for Guggenheims. I never get anything, but I don't lose anything either. I'd like to be the first Country Western Singer who gets a Guggenheim. It would feel so good.

DEVIL: Well, you couldn't lose if you had The Moon's shoes. They make all men love you.

3RD BEETHOVEN: What about all women, Devil? Have you got something up your sleeve?

DEVIL: Now don't betray your Jesuitical background, Monk. The Cowboy knows what's he doing. You and I can splice the meaning down to threads if you like but leave the Cowboy alone.

(The Monk shrugs and walks off stage. The Blue Moon Cowboy exits from the other side and The Devil goes to the center of the stage.

DEVIL: That Jesuit monk who calls himself Beethoven The Third is too clever for his own good. I've got to trick everyone this time, or I just don't think my life will be worth living. Yes, of course The Moon's shoes will make all *men* love whoever wears them, according to the magic of The King of Spain. That's what I want, the love of me. Not women. Women are fools. Why would anyone want their love? The Moon included. She's such a fool that I wouldn't even try to seduce her. The thought repels me. But if I had her shoes, her power, the gift of the night. The love of all men, and the worship of some. I could finally rest. Yes, there are lots of stories about how I fell from Grace, how I was flung out of heaven, into the punishment of this world below. And part of my hell has been this desert heat, the unrelenting sun, the lack of moisture, the light of day too bright. If I had The Moon's shoes, I would always be walking through night, through darkness, through the coolness and moisture of the world. And I would have the love of all men. I could laugh for the very brilliance of this plan. Laugh at that Fool who flung me out of heaven, saying that it was not appropriate for men to love other men. Not natural. Together He and I should have been. The perfect couple. Father and Son. Lovers. Angels together. Or gods together. But now, He is beyond all that. Well, He is a fool, and what does He have? Nothing. But a weak world on His hands. While I? I might have The Moon's shoes, if I can get one of these fools to steal them for me.

(The third Beethoven, still seeming to conduct a soundless piece of music, enters the stage, smiling fatly.)

3RD BEETHOVEN: Ah, Devil, I think I know what you are up to. Trying to delude that poor boy, The Blue Moon Cowboy; do you think he likes men better than women?

DEVIL: (in a jocular tone) I have heard that all cowboys love only their horses.

3RD BEETHOVEN: Ah, Devil, you do have delightful ideas. That one appeals to me much more than pederasty.

DEVIL: You are a vulgar creature, Beethoven. But unfortunately you understand me all too well. I am wondering what I can offer you to keep your mouth shut? After all, you don't care about The Moon and her shoes, do you? Surely, you couldn't care if I can trick them away from her?

3RD BEETHOVEN: But I am thinking of all the possibilities, Devil. I think I am wise enough not to want all men or all anything to love either you or me. Love is such an undependable emotion. And of course it causes so much trouble. No, I want listeners, I think, and even then, I wonder if listening does not eventually lead to a need for silence? But your tricks amuse me, Devil. After all, you did try to have a rather wicked relationship with Our Father in Heaven. I think we worshippers owe you a little something. If we can give it, that is.

DEVIL: Since when have you been a worshipper, Beethoven? Just because you wear that cassock hardly makes me think you're religious.

3RD BEETHOVEN: Yes, you are right. Costumes mean little. Still, this is a costume play. And we are all in it.

DEVIL: What could I give you, Beethoven? What could I offer that might tempt you into helping me? Perhaps there is the love of one man you want, though you disclaim all?

3RD BEETHOVEN: No. Love is not what I desire.

DEVIL: Sex?

3RD BEETHOVEN: No, not sex either. Maybe there is nothing I desire. Except a little fun at your expense.

DEVIL: Well, perhaps I can provide that without losing my game entirely?

3RD BEETHOVEN: We shall see, we shall see. Is this called a pact with the Devil? Our little quibble, here? (And he walks off stage, still seeming to conduct an invisible orchestra.)

(The Devil sits down and beckons for a pair of white gloves to pour him a drink. As the drink is poured, it hisses and steam rises out of the glass. The Devil smiles and drinks the steaming potion. The sound of horses' hooves is heard offstage, and as they approach, galloping, a great cloud of dust is created in the distance. The Moon has begun to rise over the stage and in the moonlight the dust appears to be illuminated. A character who has not been introduced and who is not wearing or holding a flower mask runs on stage. He is dressed in dusty riding clothes and wears a beatup cowboy hat.)

MESSENGER: (shouting) Pony Express. Pony Express. Here with a special delivery letter for G. Washington, Pres. Are you G. Washington?

DEVIL: (sipping his steaming drink) No. But perhaps you would like a refreshing drink before you continue your journey. G. Washington has been building a bar in a local saloon. He's a carpenter, you know. And he probably stopped to have a few beers before coming home.

MESSENGER: No time. No time. Must hurry on. Have another important message to deliver further west. For The Gunslinger. And one way out West in Los Angeles, for a Charles Bukowski.

DEVIL: Actually, I think Mr. Bukowski is here tonight. Hank, are you still out there? The Rider from The Pony Express has a message for you.

(Bukowski walks on stage and the messenger gives him a package wrapped in plain brown paper. Bukowski mumbles, "Smut, probably more smut from those pansy magazine editors who want me to publish with them.")

DEVIL: Well, then will you leave Mr. Washington's letter with me? I'll deliver it to him.

MESSENGER: Are you a representative of the U.S. Post Office?

DEVIL: No, but Mr. Bukowski, here, is. Why don't you give it to him, and then between us we can get it to Mr. Washington?

(The messenger hands the letter to Bukowski and runs off stage where the sound of galloping hooves is heard once again. Bukowski hands the letter to the Devil and says, "It is as safe in your hands as in mine," and goes off stage to open his package.)

DEVIL: I wonder what is in this little document. Let's see if we can steam it open with this drink. (He beckons for the white gloved hands to pour another draught of the steaming potion into his glass, and as it is steaming he holds the letter up over it and gradually nudges open the sealed flap of the envelope.) Ah ha. Fortunate choice of drinks tonight. I wonder if poor old George is tying one on at the Golden Eagle Saloon? Let's see, what does this letter say? Hmmmmmmm. It seems to be from The Moon, his daughter, herself. Wonder what trouble she's in now, and what she needs daddy for. Hmmmmm. (he reads aloud)

Dear Daddy, I think I have fallen in love with a mechanic who works on Ferraris here in the South. He is black, but I have never felt that colour should make any difference. Am thinking of marriage. Would you send one of your secretaries to help me arrange things, and any instructions on what I should do on this happy occasion?
      Love,
      Diane

Well, well. I wonder if perhaps this letter couldn't just get lost for about a week, while I go down to see Miss Moon as her father's secretary. Or better yet, perhaps I could send The Blue Moon Cowboy? I know! An even better plan! We will make sure that the letter gets to G. Washington tonight, while he's a little drunk and then perhaps he will take my advice to send The Blue Moon Cowboy himself. Oh, yes, I think they will all fall right in with my plans.

(Weaving on stage comes G. Washington, trying to walk straight and act very dignified, as he knows he is a little drunk.)

DEVIL: Mr. Pres., a letter has come for you by Pony Express.

GEORGE WASHINGTON: Thank you, sir. I don't believe I know your name, do I?

DEVIL: Friend. Goodson Friend, at your service. A travelling preacher to these parts. Looking for innocence in the desert and some ears who want to hear the Word of God.

GEORGE WASHINGTON: Um, not much of a religious man, myself. Always thought the church was for women. But my daughter nor my wife either took much to the church. Still, it is another form of order. And Order, Sir, is something the world needs.

DEVIL: A wise man. I can see how your position is dignified by such sage thoughts.

(Devil hands him the letter. Washington opens it and reads.)

GEORGE WASHINGTON: My, my, I'm a bit fuzzed in the head, but I think this letter says my daughter is getting married to a black Ferrari mechanic and wants my help. A secretary. Now who can I send?

DEVIL: Might I be of aid, Sir? Your daughter is The Moon, isn't she?

GEORGE WASHINGTON: Yes, that's right. All men love her.

DEVIL: An enviable reality, Sir. And I am thinking in particular of a very genteel young man I met on my travels who worships your daughter from afar. In fact, when I left him a few days ago he had been writing an ode to celebrate her beauty. He is a writer, and thus I would think could become a perfect secretary.

GEORGE WASHINGTON: Well, who is this admirable young man, Mr. Friend? Is he available? At hand?

DEVIL: I think so. (He waves his hand, and a puff of smoke explodes. When the smoke disappears, The Blue Moon Cowboy is standing onstage looking a little dazed.)

BLUE MOON COWBOY: Gosh, I was just finished writing my ode to The Moon and I passed out. Where am I?

DEVIL: Right here at The Society For Western Flowers, Sir. I have summoned you for a privileged commission. How would you like to be the secretary to The Moon as she prepares for her marriage?

BLUE MOON COWBOY: Her marriage?

DEVIL: That's right. It would give you an opportunity to offer her your praise and sing your songs and read your love poems to her in person, as well as helping her in this big event of her life.

BLUE MOON COWBOY: But would I be worthy? I need a new pair of boots. Another hat. I only have a dozen of these shirts. My tailor wouldn't have time to make another dozen this month.

DEVIL: Ah, Cowboy, it is your services, not your body she needs. Surely, one pair of Tony Lamas boots is enough for anyone?

(The Blue Moon Cowboy looks at him forlornly. Sighs and nods.)

GEORGE WASHINGTON: Fine then. Here's the address. Apply to my secretary in the morning for travel funds and good luck. I'll leave a list of instructions for you to take with you. Good night, now. I've had a long day.

(He exits somewhat slowly and more soberly.)

DEVIL: Do you realize, Blue Moon Cowboy, this is our big chance? You can win The Moon over and she will sponsor you on TV, on Grand Ole Opry; you can live in Nashville. But in exchange for this big favor I've done you, I want one thing. I want you to convince The Moon to give you her shoes. As a gesture of good luck for your new career. I think she'll be so wrapped up in getting married that it won't be hard. And remember, women are vain. You understand that a little yourself. Tell her it isn't right for her to be getting married in an old pair of shoes. Ask her to give them to you for luck and promise you'll reward her by bringing her fame with your songs, all dedicated to The Moon. She's so innocent (aside to the audience, hissed whisper, "stupid") (he simpers at The Blue Moon Cowboy) ahem, that she doesn't know her actual fame.

BLUE MOON COWBOY: Devil, I still don't think she'll give up those magic shoes. Besides, what do you want with them?

DEVIL: My boy, my boy, that is none of your business. Haven't I done the impossible? Given you a job with The Moon, approved of by her father, and practically set you up in Tony Lamas boots for life. Surely, a poet understands fidelity and the fact that he owes a little something for this kind of fortune respecting his art?

BLUE MOON COWBOY: (sighing) Of course, Sir. You're right. I'll do my best. But I don't think she will give them to me. Though I have started to compose a ballad called, "Just give me your Shoes, and I'll give you my Heart."

DEVIL: You see, you are inspired! You will succeed. The Moon is a sentimental fo . . . . . . I mean, woman. She will give you the shoes, I am sure.

(All exit from stage. A musical interlude occurs during which everyone eats a little, drinks a little, flirts a little. The night is pleasant. And The Moon, in fact, is full and overhead. After this interlude the play resumes with the light focusing briefly on Ludwig V. Lunar, who is still holding "The Long Note," though almost no one notices it anymore, and he is looking more frazzled and degenerate than ever since he has been holding the note for about an hour. Enter on stage, George Washington and The King of Spain.)

Act II

KING OF SPAIN: George, old man, I cannot believe what you are telling me. That my goddaughter, your natural daughter, Diane, The Moon, has given away her magic shoes to a country western singer called The Blue Moon Cowboy. How did this remarkable event occur? How could you have let this happen?

GEORGE WASHINGTON: It is a regrettable story, and yes partly my fault. A man calling himself Goodson Friend, whom I now have reason to believe is the very Devil himself, met me one night after a hard day's work and a little drinking with a letter from my daughter saying she wanted to be married and that she needed a secretary. He materialized this young man who said he worshipped my daughter, and I sent him off with instructions. He was rather a dandy, and I suppose he was in the pay of The Devil. He must have convinced her that she needed new shoes for her wedding (she was always a little shaky on the subject of not taking off those shoes). Now, of course, the man won't marry her, and she is desolate. Nobody would; not without her magic shoes. She is, after all, not as young as most men would fancy. The worst thing is that I think this cowboy was sincere, just dumb. He only wanted to write songs to her and make it big in the Nashville scene. I think he agreed to get the shoes for The Devil. God knows what The Devil will do with them.

KING OF SPAIN: Yes, God *does* know what he will do with them. That was the source of their little quarrel long ago. The Devil loves men. Carnally. And now with the magic shoes which will make all men love the wearer, he will finally be in 7th heaven.

GEORGE WASHINGTON: The Devil's a pervert?

KING OF SPAIN: Well, what else do you expect The Devil to be?

GEORGE WASHINGTON: And aided by my daughter?

KING OF SPAIN: Of course not. But I was worried about her vanity from the beginning. And I was also worried about her softness. She is a sentimental thing. She probably was touched by The Blue Moon Cowboy's love for her. Still, you'd think she'd have enough sense of self-preservation not to give those shoes away. It is not as if you and I have not warned her all of her life. The question is what are we going to do? The world will be in trouble if Diane cannot walk across the sky every night. And the world will certainly be in trouble with a Devil Pederast wearing The Moon's shoes and bedeviling all men who think of themselves as lovers.

(Enter on stage the 3rd Beethoven, still seeming to conduct his soundless orchestra.)

3RD BEETHOVEN: Well, so The Devil did it, eh?

KING OF SPAIN: What do you know about this, Beethoven? Surely, you can't have been so perverse as to help him out with this?

3RD BEETHOVEN: Oh, no. In fact, I told him I'd cheat him out of The Moon's shoes if I could. And I think I might have a plan. That is, if we can get that fool, The Blue Moon Cowboy, to help us out again. After all, he must feel a bit rotten by now, realizing what he's done. I doubt if he would notice the waning of The Moon for a year or so, but surely he will see how sad she has become now that her black Ferrari mechanic won't marry her!

KING OF SPAIN: Well, what do you suggest?

3RD BEETHOVEN: The usual. Get The Devil at his own game. We need a beautiful boy to seduce The Devil and get The Moon's shoes away from him. And I have a devilish little idea of my own, which will chagrin The Devil even more, if it works. Let's get Diane, The Moon, to disguise herself as a young boy and do the seducing!

KING OF SPAIN: That *is* a devilish idea. Probably not so easy for her either. I am her godfather. I don't know if she is up to it.

3RD BEETHOVEN: Surely, King of Spain, you want Diane to learn her lesson and if she gets her shoes back, she needs to be impressed by the seriousness of the situation. It will make it a lot harder for her to do this again. Shouldn't she have to struggle a little to retain her magical powers?

KING OF SPAIN: That's a rather Jesuitical idea, I think. And I don't know that the idea of struggling and magic aren't contradictory. But still, I think you are also talking about poetic justice, and surely that is something that Diane ought to be involved with, since it is part of her destiny.

3RD BEETHOVEN: OK, then. Will you summon her?

(The King of Spain takes an orange out of his pocket. He peels it with his golden pen knife and a golden bird flies out of it and into the desert. He calls to the bird, "Bring The Moon, Feathered Orange." Instantly, as the bird disappears The Moon stands onstage. Without her shoes, she has no radiance, and she once again appears to be the aging queen orginally assigned to the role of Diane with his/her pansy mask askew over his/her shoulders.)

3RD BEETHOVEN: This is going to be tricky for sure. He/she doesn't look young and beautiful. I wonder what The Devil particularly likes? (He muses more to himself than to the others.)

KING OF SPAIN: Goddaughter, Diane, we have summoned you tonight to work for your own destiny.

DIANE: I'm such a failure. What could I possibly do to help things?

KING OF SPAIN: First, stop crying. Then listen to me and to this smart Jesuit, here, Old Beethoven. First of all, we have to get those shoes back. The world is not the same without The Moon walking the sky each night. You have a duty beyond your own pleasure to be The Moon, beloved of all men. So, we have a plan. You are going to have to convincingly disguise yourself as a young and beautiful boy, and you are going to have to seduce The Devil and make him give you back the shoes.

DIANE: That's ridiculous. I could never look young or beautiful. Especially to that fiend. He would only ridicule me. And besides, he's not going to give those magic shoes away. He knows what they're worth. He is not foolish, as I am.

KING OF SPAIN: You knew what they were worth, Goddaughter, but you gave them away.

DIANE: But, it's not the same.

KING OF SPAIN: Yes, it is. You were tricked. And he will be tricked. It is the only way to remedy the situation.

DIANE: But how will I make myself young and beautiful. And more than that, how can I seduce the Devil? He has never been seduced. *He* is the seducer, himself. he would never let himself be caught.

KING OF SPAIN: He was thrown out of Heaven. He doesn't always win, Diane.

3RD BEETHOVEN: I have one magical trick I can offer. That is, the three of us, the other two Beethovens and myself. We have the brief magic of music at our command. And we can, I think, get The Blue Moon Cowboy to help us, though he isn't gay. But he must feel a little remorse and be willing to help us rectify the terrible situation he has inadvertently created.

DIANE: But what can your magic do to The Devil?

3RD BEETHOVEN: I think that we can get The Blue Moon Cowboy to write an ode to The Devil, telling him that he has fallen in love with him, and the other two Beethovens and I will put it to music, a music guaranteed to charm The Devil himself for its duration (about four minutes) and you can dress up as The Blue Moon Cowboy and sing this song to The Devil. Because you have always had a slightly androgynous body, you will be attractive to The Devil in a way that The Blue Moon Cowboy never would. He will think he has a sudden conquest from that unassailable world of macho men who dream of beautiful women and beat up queers. But you will have to get him to take off those shoes right away, as the musical charm can only last, at most, five minutes.

DIANE: What if I don't.

3RD BEETHOVEN: Then, we may have to recruit another moon. And that might be the end of one whole era of civilization. Are you ready to leave the heterosexual world behind? Are you ready for a new world where homosexuality is the norm? Where The Devil is beloved by all men? Surely this would be the final subjugation of women? This is not an Amazon world we're talking about. That Devil would be King (or Queen). And he would not permit women with equal powers in the world.

DIANE: You have just projected my dream of Hell. Yes. We must do this. And we must succeed. I have an idea myself.

(All exit from the stage. The rock group begins to play. "The Long Note" is still being performed in the background, though hardly anyone notices it. It is Beethoven's "Moonlight Sonata" which the rock group is playing. The scene changes and we now have The Devil lying on a couch in a bright red room, wearing The Moon's pearly shoes on his feet, but nothing else. Everyone in the room is also naked, and while at first there appears to be both men and women, a closer glance shows that all are men. The Blue Moon Cowboy—The Moon dressed as The Blue Moon Cowboy—enters the red room and is the only clothed person there. Actually, his/her clothes appear to be purple, as the blue under red lights is transformed.)

DIANE AS BLUE MOON COWBOY: Hello, Devil. I've come to pay my homage. I owe all my success to you. And while you may not believe it, I have begun to see some differences in myself. I cannot love The Moon any more. In fact, I do not even know if I can love women anymore. Your power is so strong that I have begun to compose songs for you. May I sing you a song?

DEVIL: (laughing) Of course, you delightful fool. Come and kiss my shoes first, though. They have brought us all what we love.

DIANE AS BLUE MOON COWBOY: (kissing the shoes) But I would really like to kiss your feet, Devil, for one of the disappointments of this whole adventure was my discovery that when I removed The Moon's shoes, her feet were not beautiful. I suppose they never quite got clean, as she was not able to take off those shoes, for centuries. And when she bathed, she could not lather her toes, smooth the skin with creams and lotions, could not lacquer her toenails. I suppose you have thought of some magic for doing this, but actually looking at those shoes, makes me suspicious of your feet. I would love to write an ode "To The Devil's Feet," instead of to cloven hooves, etc. Do you have beautiful feet, Devil? If you do, I think I could worship you forever. And I think I could forever convince all those sentimental fools, who still think about The Moon and wish she were walking acoss the sky each night, that The Moon's feet were dirty and ugly, and that to have her walk across the sky would actually be distracting, if they forget the magic, and repulsive, if they hadn't been hypnotized. Whereas, if I could write about your beautiful feet in contrast . . . Surely you see the power of the contrast?

DEVIL: If you were not so beautiful, Blue Moon Cowboy, I would think you were trying out some Jesuit argument on me. Who needs to see God's feet?

DIANE AS BLUE MOON COWBOY: Well, there is a lot of literature about clay feet, if not dirty feet. I guess I would just like to banish that idea once and for all.

DEVIL: First, kiss the rest of my body.

(The rock group begins to perform the magic piece of music as he/she begins erotically to kiss the body of the devil, first around the genitals, then on his nipples, back to the genitals, then around the ears and face, the nipples and genitals again, and finally he/she goes down to the shoes, and quickly removes them, as the Devil lies there, erect and excited.)

DIANE AS BLUE MOON COWBOY: Ha, ugly feet! Hooves! How could I kiss them?

(And he/she runs quickly away with the shoes. The magic of the shoes returns to The Moon as soon as he/she places them on his/her own feet. He/she looks back at The Devil with contempt and begins his/her walk through the night sky. The magic four minutes of Beethoven's music is still being played and it holds everyone still as statues before they break up into chaos, anger and tears.)

End of Masque

(The lights go on and the players all come on stage for their bows. The first Beethoven steps forward still holding "The Long Note" on his saxophone and after one hearty round of applause for him, he finally falls to the ground. A pair of gloved hands removes the saxophone from around his neck and places a pillow under his head. He simply lies there in the desert as the action continues around him.

The stout Father of Our Country rises from his table as the players take their seats in the audience and says, "The Masque is over. Let us enjoy ourselves.")

There is a feeling after a dramatic performance or a concert of completion, and it is often at odds with the social situation. That is, one wants silence. One wants to savour the richness of experience, of the new ideas absorbed, with all the sensations alive and humming. It is not the time for talk, especially not small talk, nor is it the time for maneuvering out of crowded halls. So, at least, here on the desert, we sat in our pleasant surroundings with no need whatsoever to hurry to cars or taxies or buses. But there was the inevitable human hum voicing opinions about the performance, the players, the play. I didn't want to hear any of it.

I sat immersed in my own thoughts. What was to be the nature of the new quest, the new journey? The masque seemed to imply that my journey is a daily renewal, a daily movement of self through the universe to fulfill an expectation. What did The Moon's journey across the sky each night have to do with Love, Sex, or Romance? Where was the balance, symbolized by the two sexes, yet so constantly frustrated that the human mind looked to answers like homosexuality and celibacy? Had the masque simply been a summary of past journeys, rather than a prediction of future ones?

This reverie was interrupted by the aging queen, who had played the part of Diane in the play, wearing the pansy mask over his/her face, who came up to my table. "Diane," he/she said, "I wanted to tell you how honored I was to perform your role tonight."

I hate such situations. I know the person complimenting me is sincere, but what can I say? A denial of the compliment seems rude. An acceptance seems banal and almost rude as well. I was slightly amused at this inversion of my own intentions committed by our President, G.W., and I really didn't want to insult anybody. I said in return, "And I was honored by your fine performance of the role," but what I really wanted to ask was "Why do you reject your sexuality? Is it because you are afraid of making a choice? Of the inevitable? Of reality being so punishing, once a choice is made?"

I guess I do see homosexuals as I see suicides, people so afraid of making choices that they destroy themselves rather than risk making a mistake. The pansy retreated, and I saw him/her walking over to Charles Bukowski's table. Good, I thought. He can deal with this situation better than I can. When you're drunk, everybody must look the same.

A pair of white gloves came to my table and handed me a note. "Please join me at my table. You do not have to talk, if you do not wish. G. Washington, Pres."

I got up and began to wend my way through the large garden area filled with tables and people with flower masks. Many of them smiled and nodded at me, and I tried to seem friendly, though I really wished that they were all gone. Or I thought I did. All of my life I've had problems maintaining some balance with society. When I am alone, I feel a desperate need for people. When surrounded, all I can think of is getting away, being alone.

Behind the garden I could occasionally see the glass structures, glinting as they reflected the firelight, the candles, the glitter of the crowded garden. Was it a city, a palace, a sculpture? Did it matter? Was it only a stage setting for this play which I seemed to have written for myself?

When I arrived at The President's table, he was petting his big orange cat who seemed to have no particular concern that the dalmatian was sitting at the table. Maybe the dog was a person to the cat, not an animal. After all, the dalmatian had driven the Oldsmobile. And he wore Tony Lamas boots. I noticed he was drinking something that looked like bourbon. From a glass. I said to him, "I hope you're not going to drink too much if we have to drive back tonight." He looked disdainfully at me. I had never yet heard him say a word, other than when he ran up to The President and conveyed the message that the title of the masque had been changed from "Looking For The King of Spain" to "The Moon Loses Her Shoes."

George Washington said, "Don't worry, Diane. The next part of your journey will be alone. And it will not begin tonight, for you still have not discovered what your quest is, have you?"

"No," I said, "I am more puzzled now than when I arrived."

"I can see that you want some time for thinking. I guessed as much, which is why I called you up here. You may leave through the back exit behind this table. Take a torch with you. Wander the glass, or any path you can find. You will be safe. Mother will not allow anything to happen to you."

"Mother?" All at once I thought of the big rattler I had seen curled up on the rug that afternoon. "Mother" would take care of me? Yipes, with that rattlesnake following me around I didn't really have much of an urge to go out into the night or to explore or, for that matter, even to get away from all these people.

"Actually," I said, "I think I'd like to sit here and talk to you. After all, I have been thinking for years as it is, and still have not seen the path which seems to be the chosen one. Can we have a conversation about this now?"

"Because if you stay here now, others will come to talk to you as well. And then thinking will be impossible."

"Perhaps I don't want to think right now, but simply to respond to this fantasy, this sensation of needing to locate reality."

"Very well. Here comes Ludwig V. Lunar. Hello, Ludwig. Your performance was immaculate as usual, if I may say so. It is a testimony to your genius that the present President of the United States would recognize your musical gifts. Awards go mainly to the mediocre."

"Thank you, President Washington. I am honored to be a member of The Society for Western Flowers. Did I hear you talking about an Awards Ceremony later on?"

"Oh, yes, there is one scheduled. We are awarding prizes to outstanding poets. Ludwig, allow me to introduce you to my daughter, Diane, who wrote tonight's masque."

"How do you do, Miss Moon. I understand that you know my idol, La Monte Young, a composer we've honored many times at meetings of The Society for Western Flowers. I recently made a pilgrimage to the log cabin in Idaho which has been enshrined as his birthplace. In fact, it was while there that I conceived 'The Long Note.' That's why I attribute it to him."

"Ah," said George, "our revered member of The Society for Western Flowers, Robert Duncan, says that there is no *original* art. That all art is derivative, constantly manufacturing new artifacts out of old. A pity that Mr. Duncan could not be present tonight. An early play of his features one of The Devil's favorite characters."

I knew this was a reference to "Faust Foutou" but certainly would never have connected it with this masque. George was a wise old bird. In more ways than one.

"I wonder," I ventured, "if he would have regarded the portrayal of The Devil as a homosexual as ultimately foolish?"

George smiled his Mona Lisa smile. Ludwig wanted to talk about La Monte Young and his music, and I told him of a recent performance of "The Well Tuned Piano" which I had heard in New York at the new studio. It was only then that I realized the body of Ludwig V. Lunar was still lying on the stage in front of us, and that somehow we must be talking to his spirit. I was trying to figure out how to say something which wouldn't sound utterly stupid when, to my rescue, Charles Bukowski came up to our table and said, "Well, Ludwig, up to your old tricks again? Remember when we played on the team together? What a halfback you were! This is a new gig for you, isn't it? Out-of-body travel? Where'd you learn this?"

"Actually, said Ludwig, "there are several of me and I have only recently learned how to manifest them all. Diane's play captured the right idea by giving my part three actors. I know now that there are at least three of me, but so far I only know how to be one at a time. To depart from my body is the first step, but it is hard to have character without a body, and so I am on a quest, a journey, too, Diane, looking for a way to transcend myself. I have left Ludwig V. Lunar's body lying there because he almost used it up in performing "The Long Note." It has to be recharged. But his spirit is still whole and I have floated it out of his body, that is, floated myself out of my body. This problem of understanding three selves does become confusing at times."

"Hey, man, you're being cagey. Not telling us the secret. How do you get out of your body?" Bukowski seemed almost ready to start composing a poem at that moment since he was obviously enjoying the strange situation immensely.

Ludwig said, "I'm sorry, Buk. I just can't tell you. It has nothing to do with John Cage. But I think it has something to do with abstinence."

"Holy shit, I knew it would be something impossible!" Bukowski just stood smiling, and I could hear the poem bubbling inside of him. I wondered what he was doing here, since I thought he never left L.A., being so addicted to the horse races at Santa Anita. Still, poets get around, and since I am such a Bukowski fan, I didn't really care too much about the reasons that got him here. However, my silent question was answered just then by our President.

"I'm so glad you could come to emcee our Awards Ceremony. Your touch would definitely have been missed had The King of Spain been forced to do the honors. He has magic but not rhetoric. It is probably just as well that he usually remains invisible." What I have always thought Diane meant about The King of Spain is that he is silent, not invisible. She sees him, though others don't. She just never hears him.

As usual George was more perspicacious than I was. "Well, Diane," he said, "I think you should take a short walk around this garden before the Awards are presented. Remember you are the one who has to find the meaning."

By this time the magic of the play had worn off, and I had had a few more glasses of wine. I was beginning to realize that this place was not meant to frighten me, or to cause me trouble, but rather to bring me the pleasures of poetry, of fantasy, of life beyond the body. So, I excused myself from the table and walked around the bonfire behind us and saw the gigantic gate I had entered earlier. The glass caught the firelight's red & blue flames and I thought for a moment of the last scene in the masque, where the stage was flooded with red light and The Blue Moon Cowboy appeared to be purple. It had been erotic, yet repulsive at the same time, and I had been terribly relieved when the seduction was reversed and The Devil left desiring, while The Moon walked off stage in her white shoes. Why, I kept asking myself, does the body cause so much trouble? Not the body, I answered myself, but the need to merge the body and the mind. It doesn't work except for fantastic events. Ludwig V. Lunar's out-of-body travel wasn't really more exotic than my rejection of homosexuality or multiple sexual relationships. They were all our exaggerated means of trying to understand how the body and the mind come together, and to create an order that gives harmony. And, of course, music had to be some factor in all of this.

As I walked through the gates, I looked up to see if I could still see the sign BLOOD FACTORY. Actually, I was startled because not only could I see it, it was as if it were a neon sign. Dante's Hell didn't have gates like this. Now, at night, it looked more like a glamourous night club and just as I realized that, the sign began blinking on and off, on and off, just as certain big city signs do. Well, this was surely not going to let me know what my journey was. Though a devilish thought occurred to me that maybe there would be one of those marquees up there, like the ones at Ramada and Holiday Inns, which say "Welcome, Gail and Bill on your 50th," and it might just have a hint on it, such as

"Diane, West" or "Goodbye Moon." Why did I think there was another quest ahead of me anyway? Was it because I had never actually completed my previous one? What had I said to The President? That I had been searching for the perfect man, the perfect mate? That for me it was a search for completion or fulfillment? Certainly I saw sexuality as the completing of the male principle with the female and vice versa. Yet, I also believed in the lonely life, or to be more precise, I believed that one's destiny as a human is completely alone, lonely, solved only by oneself. How did this fit with my idea that a person needed a mate, that he needed to fulfill himself sexually, that when his life was balanced with male- and femaleness, he had completed himself sexually, that when his life was balanced with male- and femaleness, he had completed *himself*?

I realized that I saw this as a kind of hierarchy, the biological or combined biological-psychological needs had to be met before the being could contemplate other needs. I had always had my own version of this. I have even held moral versions of these ideas, feeling that it was a greater human act to survive poverty and become well-educated and concerned with intellectual, aesthetic or spiritual things, than to be born comfortable and move right into those "higher" concerns.

My love for classic Greek drama and for literature in that tradition comes from my feelings that it is more important to solve the problems of having murdered your father, married your mother, etc. than simply to feel unwanted or unloved or unprotected. The acting out of feelings is perhaps partly art, but perhaps it is also part of a reality we eventually have to face. Thus, I start asking myself often, not only is it important that Frank Bidart, in his poem "Ellen West," choose a woman who is literally starving herself to death, to dramatize the need to transcend the body for everyone in this culture, but also, is the person who actually decides to do this—the anorexic, who starves herself to death as an enactment of her desire to transcend her body—a greater human being than those of us who deny ourselves in moderation, in hopes that we will be in tune with the greater reality? Yet, perhaps dying is the greater reality. And perhaps sacrifice is the test of any real principle or idea. Thus, perhaps what George is telling me is that now that I have finally come from the starved, unloved, rejected, sacrificing person to a life which supplies wholeness, or a creation of self which seems whole, the next journey is the real journey. For, I had to be made whole before I could be considered a worthwhile sacrifice for whatever principle it is I believe in. Somehow as I am saying this, I feel that not everything harmonizes. Surely I am not destructive or self destructive, and yet I keep seeing the need for sacrifice. And death. I am not really a Dionysian either. I have only seen the truth of the Dionysian way. But like Ginsberg, I see it as the alternate great truth to the Apollonian way. That way denied to so many of us, born in poverty or into disruptive lives. Yet, if I start with wholeness now, then surely the Apollonian way is possible for me? How do I journey towards light and air? Away from darkness and the swamp of beginnings? What journey will I be taking, The Dionysian or The Apollonian? The desert must be the landscape for Apollo. The sun brilliant here. The air even is thin and pure. The vegetation more of mineral than of loam. Yet, The Society for Western Flowers certainly seems to be an organization concerned with transformations. There are these spectacular plants growing in the desert, which means an underground source of water, a deep spring feeding this place. That spring is Dionysian, feeding this Apollonian landscape. George Washington himself, and The King of Spain, both Apollonians. The woodsman, mechanic, carpenter, all Apollonian, bringing order and civilization.

And no, I know the temptation of thinking that if you can put the two ideas together you have perfection when all you really have is lack of choice. Choice *is* important. It means risk. It means at least 50% chance of failure. It means leaving something out because you cannot have opposites at one time. Yet, that is what I yearn for, that duality I have always spoken of; it is the spiritual duality which allows opposites to co-exist and to simultaneously be true. This is not possible in the body. You cannot be fat and thin at the same time. You cannot be blond and dark at the same time. You can cheat by saying that you put the dark nature into the fair body, etc. But that is cheating. You cannot have a blizzard and 90-degree temperature at the same time. Not in this world. And wouldn't that be a science fiction hell for everybody—a blizzard which was throwing out ice-hot snow, scalding and freezing simultaneously.

I had walked through the gate and was walking along a glass corridor which seemed to lead to a hothouse. When I reached the conservatory it was filled with camellias, bushes 8 to 10 feet high, rooted in dark humus soil. Man-made, of course, I thought. This is cheating. This is what civilization does. Bringing the garden to the desert. This is what civilization does; it cheats to make impossible results. That is what magic does. But all magic, all cheating has its rules. Thus to maintain the illusion for a long time is usually not possible. Smog around our cities is the price of autos and air conditioning. Do we want magic? Yes. Must we pay the price for it? Yes. Can we keep finding new magic, to banish the old conditions resulting from vanished illusions? Smog. Polluted rivers. Low water tables. Can we keep finding new magic? Perhaps. So, what is my journey? Should I become a scientist rather than a poet? Nonsense. For my problems would still be the same. And the choice of quest still the difficult one.

But, now I am saying the choice of quest, as if I know the possibilities. Does George think I know the possibilities? Have I always known the possibilities once I reach a certain point? And what was the allegory of the Masque? Was The Moon a personification of Good and The Devil a personification of Evil? Was The Moon a personification of humanity, or foolishness, or weakness? And, if so, why wasn't The Devil also a personification of weakness, of humanity, of foolishness? Didn't he fall as fast as The Moon? In fact, he didn't have anyone to help him, as she did. Was he really the hero of the masque? Perhaps if it had had another act? But we left him with his chaos and his boy lovers and his folly. There is no implication that The Moon was going to get her husband, the black Ferrari mechanic either. Just a new sense of the importance of her inevitable purpose, which surely she will betray again after another 1,000 years of walking the sky.

And the ending seemed pretty pat, but I guess that is the nature of allegory. The Moon representing the heterosexual world, The Devil representing the homosexual world. Perhaps the masque was one last magical rite to stave off the holocaust of a total male world, of men loving men exclusively, of women becoming biologically extinct as history has tried to make them intellectually extinct. Rather effete magic, though, if that's the case.

I was standing in front of a large bush filled with candle-smooth white camellias, when I heard a hissing behind me. I jumped about a foot, as I am easily startled and had been completely in my own thoughts at the time. I was almost afraid to look, but I did, and there was Mother, the big snake, coiled up further down the passage. She was rising, and I had been taught that meant snakes were going to spring at you, and I was petrified. The hissing was getting louder and I almost expected the snake to have steam coming out of her mouth. Well, maybe this was my next journey. To be bitten by a snake and go to some underground of delirium until I died or was rescued. This thought suddenly made me realize that I wasn't as frightened as I thought I would be. "Oh, shut up," I said. "You're supposed to protect me, Mother." Magic words? Charm the snake? I guess so, because Mother began to relax and uncoiled and slid away down the corridor. What do you expect, Diane, I said to myself. This is still the night before your journey. That snake I don't trust, but it wasn't your time yet.

And I certainly didn't have any idea about my new journey either. I think I knew that I had to choose an underground journey, one which offered in exchange for death and its rituals, rebirth and a new life. But I was afraid of death and did not really believe that promise of rebirth would be kept. And like most Victorian heroines, I was reluctant to make choices. Inevitable choices. I, like most of them, was a master at not making any choice, at hanging around for the world to make proper choices for me and then to make it seem as if I had chosen correctly all along. It has always been amazing to me that many people see inevitable actions in my life as choices. I have had so few choices. And I have been so reluctant to make each one. I have lived a life of exigency, one that has forced most things upon me, thus I am well prepared to accept crisis and catastrophe, but completely unprepared to accept civilized choices.

No wonder I love those Victorian novelists, Hardy, Eliot, Dickens, Austen. How preferable the world of Esther Summerson, Tess or Dorothea or any such heroines to mine—where they can make almost no real choices, can only make the best of bad situations. That is what I have been trained to do. Make the best of bad situations, and enjoy the freedom of knowing that I did not cause those situations. What about choice? I might cause the bad situation itself, if I had choices. And it is so much less possible to make the best of a situation when you hate yourself for having caused it. All of those novelists' heroines had the moral joy of knowing that they did *not* cause their own problems. What an incredible freedom. How blessed we are in affliction. And thus the beauty of the Dionysian way. Through death there is rebirth. But only if you did not cause your own death. Only if you did not squander your life. Only if that death were inflicted upon you. Yes, if Oedipus had known the man he killed in anger in the pass was his father, his killing would have been very different. Had he knowingly consorted with his mother sexually, how different his fate. The Dionysian cannot be chosen. It is the means of salvation provided in a harsh world where suffering is inflicted, and not one where it is chosen.

Do I have a choice then? Yes. If there is destiny, can one choose? And can one make a mistake? Which way am I destined for? Have I confused destiny with passive behavior?

As a baby in his crib, Apollo strangled the two great serpents. Had his spirit come upon me for a moment when I shooed Mother away? Or was I simply familiar enough by now with aging female dragons, having been one myself for some years now, to know how harsh words waste them? Or was it all part of a spell? Mother was there to remind me, while protecting me. To bring me out of the flowers, into the world of breath. Her hissing. My expectations of steam. Yes, I had been married to The

Devil once, and he still frightened me with his sexuality and the pain I felt when I thought about him. Naked, except for The Moon's shoes.

I walked back through the glass corridor out past a grove of palms, through the rose garden and back to the gate which was flashing the words, BLOOD FACTORY, in red neon. The Blue Moon Cowboy was standing by the gate, humming to himself.
"Hello, Cowboy," I said.
"Hello, Diane. I do love you, you know."
"I believe you. Though I don't believe most people who say that. I believe in the word. That is, poetry as the word. I believe in it more than I believe in the body. The mind and the body cannot be reconciled. Except temporarily. That is the futility of the quest for body's harmony with mind. They constantly contradict each other just to prove each other. The question is, does the word come from the mind, or the body?"

Ignoring this question, The Blue Moon Cowboy touched my shoulder and said, "I think I know what you are looking for, Diane."

"Tell me."

"You are looking for beauty through the word, beyond love, beyond the body, beyond men and women. You despair of homosexuality because basically you hate sexuality. You accept male-female coupling as survival, as biology, as eating in order not to die. But you have never loved sex for its own sake and you see that reality triumphant in homosexuality. And you are right, in your quest, to want to go beyond the body, beyond sex or even food. The trap of your youth was that sexual urge invading your life. The trap of your middle age is food and the longing of the palate invading your life. The word battles with each of these elements on the chain of fulfillment. Peter Quince at the Clavier spoke to you before you even knew what you were thinking. I play a version of his music and that's why I love you. I know you are my perfect listener."

"Thank you, Blue Moon Cowboy," I said. And that was that. He was the poet.

George Washington was sitting at his table with Charles Bukowski, and though I didn't think George really was laughing, his lips seemed curved up a bit more than his usual Mona Lisa smile. I was glad Bukowski was here. He was/is the truest of Dionysian poets, his life and work a constant illustration of rebirth from the death of the deadly bourgeois world, the death that comes from genteel language and packaged foods, from cheap carpet in every room and more than one television set. From too many family vacations, and perhaps even from "family rooms." The family that prays together is stuck together. I see survival in terms of being alone, having separate rooms and separate lives. I hate community personalities, and Bukowski represented The Loner for me as much as any man. Perhaps the secret of communication is to be enough alone to need to communicate.

"Well, Diane," said Bukowski, "have you done your heavy thinking? Got any secrets to tell the world? Or have you lost your shoes again?"

I am always speechless when people I admire address me. So, I sort of simpered, hating myself and said nothing. "Hey, Pres.," said Bukowski, "let's get this show on the road, shall we?"

George lifted his bird-of-paradise which chimed once again, and as it sounded, all the flower masks also made small ringing sounds. Gradually, people began to seat themselves. The King of Spain was wearing his red opium poppy mask and again sitting at the same table with the play's George Washington, who looked even more gigantic with one of the little sweet pea girls sitting on his lap. There was no doubt in my mind this time, for she had her mask off, that those little sweet pea girls were no more than 12 years old at most. If The Blue Moon Cowboy were right, all my taboos had much more to do with my wanting to reject sex entirely than with sex itself. I should stop thinking about the whole subject. Sodomy. Pederasty. Lolita-ism. It was the Devil's temptation to make me think about that which I shouldn't.

George said, "Ladies and Gentlemen, this evening's Award Ceremony will be emceed by the Society's choice poet, Charles Bukowski."

"Thank you, Pres. Is everybody having a good time? Then, let's let on with it. Let's get on with it. Got some rules. Awards have rules. So, here they are (burp) (Bukowski is holding a Budweiser beer bottle as he has seemed to all evening.) This Moselle is pretty good for dessert wine. Ha ha ha. The rules. We are giving ten prizes for mediocrity. Oops, I mean, uh, Something Else. Actually, I wanted George to give the prizes for mediocrity because I am a traditionalist, and that is consistently what most prizes are given for. However, the Pres., our historic leader, had pointed out that poets are makers of their own traditions, and that we should and could make our own rules. We have taken the names of our prizes from the common wildflowers of the United States, and we have decided to give twelve awards. The judges for the contest, of course, were The Blue Moon Cowboy, Beethoven, The King of Spain, The Motorcyclist-Woodsman, George Washington, The Devil and Diane. Right now I'd like to introduce The Pres himself to tell you about the prizes. This whole scene may make me sick, so I'm going to drink a little beer and hope that by the time I have to give these awards I'll think everybody writes great poetry, even Manfred Anderson, that boy friend of my ex-wife's, who's afraid to send out his poems. Pansy freak. Don't know why I didn't stick with horse racing. Here's the Pres., G. Washington."

"Good evening again, friends. I'd like to begin by explaining our awards to you. In addition to these awards which will be given every five years, in the name of American Wild Flowers, I'd like to give two personal awards tonight. One of them is to our evening's Master of Ceremonies, Charles Bukowski, otherwise known as Hank Chinaski. He has been given The Orchid Award for his work. The orchids, many of which are native to the American continents, are flowers which have richly developed sexual lives.

They are also among the longest-lived flowers, often staying in fact on a plant for as long as two or three months. This has given them an odd place in American life, the flower most often chosen for corsages, guaranteed not to wilt throughout long hot struggling evenings. They are expensive at the florists and considered very difficult to grow in the home. Mr. Bukowski is one of our most original poets writing today. His work presents the Dionysian myth at its purest, and it comes from the deepest, most secret and rich jungles in the human psyche. It is beloved by serious readers of poetry and generally scorned by the academic critics of this world.

"The second personal award I would like to give is The Pansy Award to Diane Wakoski for her continued belief in The Society for Western Flowers and the celebration of it, of me, of our honored judges, The Blue Moon Cowboy, Beethoven, The Motorcyclist-Woodsman, and herself, The androgynous Moon.

"The first of our awards is The Sedum or 'Live Forever' Award. This will be given to a poet who in the Society's judgment has produced work of profound originality, helping to change the shape and character of American poetry, and contributing to the tradition of Emily Dickinson, Walt Whitman, William Carlos Williams, Wallace Stevens, and Robinson Jeffers.

"The second of our awards will be The Trientalis Borealis or 'Star Flower' Award. It will go to a poet who, in our judgment, has most captured the imagination of serious American readers of poetry.

"The third award, The Impatiens Capensis or 'Jewelweed' or 'Orange Touch-Me-Not' Award will be bestowed on a poet who has special healing powers, (as does the jewelweed, a folk remedy for poison ivy) and who also possesses magical and visionary powers.

"The fourth award, The Opuntia or 'Prickly Pear' Award will go to the author of an original long poem which attempts to explore an area previously unexplored by American poetry.

"The fifth award, The Galinsoga or 'Gallant Soldier' Award will be presented to a poet who has worked long and hard with almost no recognition for his originality and excellence.

"The sixth award, The Viola Blanda or 'Sweet White Violet' Award will be given to the singers, the beautiful voices, the poets whose grace and lyricism of voice will seduce even the most hardened listeners.

"Seventh, we will have The Solidago Gigantea or 'Goldenrod' Award. This will be presented to a poet whose voice is prolific, native, common to the land and language, and whose work, like the flower, spreads in the fields, common beauty over the countryside.

"The eighth award, The Campion or 'Sticking Cockle' or 'Night Flowering Catchfly' Award will go to a poet whose work is difficult, hard to penetrate, often repulsive to readers, but which is original and important in the landscape.

"The ninth award, The Gypsophila or 'Baby's Breath' Award will be given to poets whose voices are delicate, quiet, innocent and new. It will be a pervasive voice but one of great fragility, often unperceived because of this.

"The tenth award, The Cerastium or 'Chickweed' Award will go to new poets whose work is so special that it is observable in even the first collection of poems published. This is not a first book award, though it might appear to be so. The work must appear inevitable and distinguished because it will be carrying on observable traditions in new ways.

"The eleventh award will be The Lippia Lanceolata or 'Fogfruit' Award. This will go to a poet whose voice is deep and resonant of the past, though it is full of warning for the future.

"The final award, The Nymphoides Peltana or 'Yellow Floating Heart' Award will be given to a poet who carries on old traditions in new but subtle ways.

"Now, I will again turn this ceremony over to our Master, Charles Bukowski, the first winner of The Orchid Prize, and surely one of America's finest poets. Thank you."

Bukowski's forehead was gleaming with sweat in the firelight, and I wondered why because the night air was definitely chilly. "Thought you'd never finish, George. This all sounds like a lot of shit to me. What I want to know is can you drink an award? Can you bet with it on the races? Metaphor is a long shot in the last race, but who'd ever think that originality would beat her out?

"I want everybody to know that I didn't pick these winners. I didn't even bet on most of them. Shit, I wouldn't have thought most of them would even show. This is the masterminding of that committee of Diane's muses, The King of Spain (obviously a fraud), Beethoven, all three of him, our honored president, G.W., that character who can't read, The Motorcyclist-Woodsman (oh, excuse me, Diane. So he reads. Probably just shit like *The Inferno* or *Zen and the Art of Motorcycle Maintenance*), The Moon herself, natch, and her newest find, The Devil. That guy's always in on awards, no matter who's giving them. I wonder which one of these he took an active hand in? Hey, George, how about you letting me give one of my own awards? I could give 'The Skunk Cabbage' Award or 'The Stinkhorn' Award. I have a lot of candidates for either one of those awards. I see Diane whispering that the 'Stinkhorn' is a fungus. If I had my way, these would all be Fungus Awards. Alright, Diane, I see you protesting. Well, give me another beer, and I'll get on with it. Yeh, let's get on with it. I hope this doesn't make me puke. I wish Hemingway were here and we could get drunk together. He wouldn't go for this stuff either. Poets. Hopeless cases. All of them.

"The first award, The Sedum Award, otherwise known as The 'Live Forever' Award (shit, is this cheating) will be presented to three poets, two dead and one living. Now that doesn't make any sense, does it? To give a 'live forever' award to somebody who's dead? I said I didn't have anything to do with this crap. The Sedum Award tonight goes to Jerome Rothenberg, most recently the author of *Vienna Blood,* but also the author of *Poland 1931* and many other (it says here) great books of poems. Rothenberg makes anthologies like nobody else. In other words, for a Yid he's pretty good. Along with Jerome Rothenberg, The Sedum Award will be going to Charles Olson, the author of *The Maximus Poems,* and Frank O'Hara, author of *The Lunch Poems* (where do they get these titles? Christ, I need another beer.) Okay you guys, let's give a big hand for Jerome Rothenberg, Charles Olson, and Frank O'Hara (those last two can't hear you, but do it anyway), the winners of the first Sedum or 'Live Forever' Award in poetry."

For the first time, I saw that indeed Jerome Rothenberg, my first publisher and old friend, was here in the audience. I wondered why I hadn't noticed before. He was sitting at a table with the three Beethovens, including the spirit or out-of-body Beethoven who had performed "The Long Note" during the masque. His body was still lying on stage. In fact, at one point I'd been worried that Bukowski would step on it. But he didn't. As Rothenberg walked to the stage, I noticed something strange about him. He sort of floated and even bobbed a bit. Finally, I saw that his legs were not moving at all, that he was floating and when he turned around, to my shock, I saw that it wasn't Jerry Rothenberg at all, but a balloon which looked like Jerry. Bukowski grabbed the life-sized balloon's hand and shook it. The balloon bobbed a bit more as Bukowski said congratulations and the balloon bobbed back down into the audience and to the table with the Beethovens.

George Washington said to me, "Diane, you look worried."

"Well, why isn't Rothenberg here, and why do we have a balloon instead?"

"Simple, Diane, simple. He sent the balloon. Said he had to be at an Indian ceremony in the area and that he might drop by tomorrow. He doesn't take awards too seriously, he said, and he thought it would be better to accept even the award from The

Society for Western Flowers as an inflated rubber man than in person. He didn't mean it as an insult, Diane. Just a gesture of scepticism. Surely you understand that? I seem to remember that you once told me that you and Jerry used to talk about what absurd gestures you would dream up if you were ever to receive Pulitzers or National Book Awards."

"Well, of course . . ." But I was still a little worried.

Then Bukowski said, "Got to hand it to that Rothenberg. He knows how to receive an award. Okay, now for our Trientalis Borealis. Well, natch, who else would it go to, who else *could* it go to than America's most famous poet, Allen Ginsberg? Hiya, Allen. Come on up here and accept The Trientalis Borealis. Say, I'm really getting hooked on these latin names. Why don't we give all our poems latin names too? Out of date, I guess. Oh, well. Where is Allen? Allen, aren't you coming up to get your 'Star Flower' Award?"

At this moment, for Allen Ginsberg was definitely not in the audience, the sound of a harmonium squeezing itself heavily was heard, and a tambourine was being rattled and through the entrance gate where I last saw The Blue Moon Cowboy lounging, came a long-haired tall white-loose-flowing-garment-clad figure, jumping and rattling the tambourine. It was Peter Orlovsky, Ginsberg's lifetime companion. Behind him, was a little electric car, like those used to carry parade floats, and behind it there was in fact a kind of float, with Allen Ginsberg sitting on a white platform, squeezing away at his harmonium. The car was driven by someone who looked like Gregory Corso when he was very young, with wild curly black hair. A path was cleared to the stage, with Peter hopping about and chanting, and Ginsberg grinding the harmonium and singing, "Little Lamb, Little Lamb."

"Ha, ha," said Bukowski, "The Devil couldn't have made a better entrance. Welcome, Allen and Peter. Let's have a beer for everybody. I know you guys pretend you don't drink, but this is a special occasion. I now present you, Allen Ginsberg, The

Trientalis Borealis Award, The 'Star Flower' Award for your contributions to American poetry. Your original voice speaking out of Whitman's tradition has changed the shape and possibilities of American poetry as much as any voice in history. Even I think you're not such a bad poet, though I wish you'd throw that damn harmonium in the garbage or give it to some museum. A big hand for Allen Ginsberg."

"Thank you, Buk. But I want to make a statement. I know your intentions are good, but I want to reject the award and give it to my friend, Peter Orlovsky instead. Peter needs it. Peter deserves it because he understands America and loves her so much better than I do. Peter loves shit. He farms and appreciates all forms of manure. He thinks of it, winter and summer, and cultivates our land in Cherry Valley with it. As such, I deem him a true believer in and lover of this country, which is the shit capital of the world. I thank you for The Trientalis Borealis Award and hereby confer it on the truly deserving Peter Orlovsky, a true 'Star Flower.' "

"Well, I don't know what to say, Allen. I guess now you guys will just have to have a beer. What else is left?" Ginsberg gets back on his float and Peter starts banging his tambourine, while Allen starts wheezing on the harmonium. The electric vehicle silently, except for the music, wheels them out into the desert night. I wonder where they are going, but know they have friends everywhere.

"Well, nothing but surprises tonight." Bukowski takes a long chug-a-lug of his beer and burps like a teenager. "Guess you have to expect something a little different with these Wildflower Awards, though. Okay, now we are awarding The Impatiens Capensis or The 'Jewelweed' or The 'Orange Touch-Me-Not' Award. It is for the poet who has special healing gifts, as well as magical and visionary powers. Now this is where a lot of poets run their scams. Seems to me there are hundreds of poets pretending to these powers, with fake Ouija boards, and prep-school accented claims to visionary language. Lot of hokum. Everybody knows that you have to die first before you see visions, and most of these guys cater to their health and to some middle-American idea of success that never gives them a chance to die, to say nothing of going underground and getting reborn. Frankly, I don't think that O'Hara knew much about it either. He died for real. But then, I said it was the committee who chose those prizes, not me. Diane has some notion about O'Hara being a new Apollonian poet, discovering the movies as a replacement for the sun, rich famous people replacing the stars. These ideas of hers are pretty spacey themselves. And she does love them pansies . . ."

A voice interrupts him from the audience. It is the 3rd Beethoven. "Hey, Buk, remember that she thinks you're the greatest too. Where does that put you?"

"Alright, you Jesuit, shut up. I'm running this show. Diane's ideas are alright for a lady poet. But all she drinks is that French wine. No wonder she has those ideas. It's affected her mind."

I hate making myself seen in these situations but I felt I had to defend myself slightly. "Uh, actually, I drink a lot of California wine these days . . ."

"It's all the same, except the California juice costs more now. Still rots your brain. Not like beer. A real food. Nourishes you. Or German wine. Pure vitamins."

Various members of the audience have started to call "Boo," and "hiss," and Bukowski acknowledges their protests. "Alright, alright, let's get on with this show. So, I was saying this Impatiens Capensis Award is going to be presented to a genuine poet of Vision. And I am proud to announce the winner, Robert Duncan. Come on up here, Bob, let the audience see a real magician."

The Devil, from the masque, stands up and starts to walk on stage.

"Wait a minute, Devil," Bukowski holds up his hand, "I called for Robert Duncan, not for you."

The Devil smiles and beams around at the audience, then leers at Bukowski. "Mr. Duncan asked me to accept his award for him this evening. He and some friends of mine have gone to a special showing of Kenneth Anger's new film, "Lucifer Rising" in Paris where Isis and Osiris will be hosting a party afterwards. He felt this award, as much as he appreciates it, not having any money attached to it, could be accepted without his presence. And naturally, I volunteered to help him out. He and I are old acquaintances. I was hoping that if I did this little favor for him I might have a chance to get a little better acquainted in the future. So, in his name, I accept The Impatiens Capensis Award. He has asked me to read these words from 'Passages 6' as a response. So, if you'll sit down, Mr. Bukowski, I'll take over the stage for a bit."

The Devil puts on a mask which he has in a bag, which looks like the face of Robert Duncan and he reads:

>   This way below is the way above
> the mouth of the cave or temple growing moist
>   shining,   to allow   the neophyte
>   full entrance.
>   The body of the poem, aroused,   having
>   what mouths?
> It wont smear, it can be
>   moved, can move,   but
>   no word, it's that clear,   is
>   soft, shit, painty •   Can consonants
>   so crawl or blur   to give . . .
>   contrive to imitate juices, excretions, the body's
>   spit?
>   beyond how wet the air will
>   come and carry these vowels?
>   these dentals, labials, the tongue
>   so adamantly insists upon?
>   this rrr   to be a river
>   and I place here, my air;
>   this block with   ⬚E
>
>   for elefant

                              is throne,   is soft, and
        as far as I get in the play

            runs down   •

                                                              (4/1/64)
                        runs away with me
            and I enter the wave of it.
        How long have I been waiting,
                            the language, the sea, the body
                rising above
                            sleep
            above

                            and leaves us
            fallen back
                            above sleep   •
the moon taking over tides of the mind,
pulling back
        whatever cover love had
until the reefs upon which we lie are exposed,
    the green water going out over
                            the rock ledges,
body upon body
        turning keys as the tide turns
and reaching up into . . .

    In the curve of the dark
            the light strives
                    where they come
    . . . the roll of the returning waters
        over the stone stretches
                            remotely
reaching us.

As the Devil finishes reading he bows, leers again at Bukowski, and walks toward his seat in the audience. Bukowski takes the stage again.

"Oh, you Devil, you. Now, give me another beer, and let's get on with the show. The next award looks to me like another one of Diane's little pansy numbers. It is The Opuntia or 'Prickly Pear' Award, and it will be given to a poet whose long poem attempts to explore an area previously unexplored by American poetry. I don't know why anybody would want to read or write long poems. What I say is why not write a novel or short story if you're going to get long-winded? But I'm just the D.J. tonight. They should have gotten Rodney Dangerfield to do this number on his way to Vegas. Just think how much respect a bunch of poets would give him. Probably too much. Probably so much that he wouldn't want to come. Have you ever thought about where Rodney Dangerfield would be if everybody gave him respect? Up shit's creek, that's where. Anyway, The Opuntia Award tonight goes to Ed Dorn, author of *Gunslinger,* a long poem which attempts to present a dramatic narrative which embodies the study of phenomenology and phenomenological linguistics. Don't ask me why anybody'd want to do that in a poem, but Dorn has done it, and let's have a big round of applause for Ed Dorn, the author of *Gunslinger.* Where are you, Ed Dorn?"

I also wondered what would happen, because I hadn't seen Dorn in the audience either. Actually, I hadn't seen any poets I recognized other than Bukowski earlier in the evening. I wondered if that were because most poets aren't interested in other poets' work, and this play had been billed as being written by me, even though, as I told you, George himself obviously wrote it and attributed it to me. I began to wonder how Ginsberg happened to materialize on cue, also. After all, you can't just be passing through the desert and stop off to get an award on the way to the movies. The timing of his arrival was so perfect that obviously something had been staged. Maybe when George Washington sent me out to wander around, it was to give me a chance to see all these poets who might have been waiting in some other part of the glass structure. Still, if they were there, why didn't they come to the masque? Did this have anything to do with George's idea about my quest, about what I should think about my search, my life as a poet? His Pansy Award had pleased me, but somehow seemed sort of like a door prize given to the first guest to arrive, rather than a real award. I had no doubt that Bukowski's award, The Orchid Prize was real. But what about mine? If George said that I wrote the play, then he might also say that I gave myself the award. Of course, most awards are really meaningless and given by friends anyway. I've always said that. But then I've always longed for a Pulitzer Prize, while saying that. So maybe George created this situation so that I would have to admit finally how unreal getting any prize is, and how meaningless and what a random and unduplicatable accomplishment it was.

I heard the sound of horses' hooves, looked towards the gate, and saw Ed Dorn come through, leading a horse. I supposed it was Claude Levi-Strauss, otherwise known as Hi-Digger, and I realized when I saw them that this was the actor and his horse who had played the rider from the Pony Express in the masque. He had rushed in so fast during the play that I hadn't paid any attention to him, and his back had been turned, as well as being dusty and dressed in old fashioned clothes. Still, it made me feel foolish, and I wondered why unlike the rest of the players, he hadn't joined the audience to drink and talk after the play. Right now, he looked dusty and tired too, as if he'd actually been riding around out there on the desert. This was getting to be ridiculous.

Bukowski waved his beer bottle. "Welcome, welcome, and congratulations on your Opuntia Award."

Dorn ambled over to Bukowski, looking weary. "Has anyone seen Hughes?"

"Howard, you mean? Hell, he's dead. What do you want him for?"

With resignation, Dorn said, "That's part of my journey. I'm not searching for meaning, ontological or otherwise. I'm searching for money. How much does this award pay?"

"All you can drink tonight. Good grub here too. But I think our Pres. has a cash flow problem. Actually, I think there's the possibility of another form of consciousness here tonight too. Ask one of the Beethovens."

"Well, thanks a lot for The Opuntia Award. Hope in the future you get some guy to endow it. Maybe you should be looking for Hughes too?"

"Howard? He's dead. Okay, okay, let's get on with this show. See you later, Ed. Let me know if you find Lil. Shit, there are a lot of these awards. I guess if you're not giving money, you can afford to be generous. The fifth award, The Galinsoga or 'Gallant Soldier' Award, for a poet who's worked diligently for years with little recognition other than publication, tonight, is to be given to David Ignatow."

Again, I wondered where David Ignatow would be stashed or what trick would produce him.

Bukowski said, "We have called David Ignatow on the phone tonight and are putting the mike up to the phone so that you can hear his acceptance. As usual, Mr. Ignatow had a day job and a night job and couldn't leave New York for the presentation of awards."

George Washington holds the receiver of the telephone up to a microphone set up on his table. We hear Ignatow's voice through the amplified phone. "Hello?"

George Washington says, "Hello, David. We're calling tonight to present you with The Galinsoga or 'Gallant Soldier' Award for poetry. You have many fans here in the audience, including Diane Wakoski, who writes about you as a Dionysian poet and as one of the only truly American existential poets. We would like to add our congratulations and say how much your wry and witty poems have meant to us over the years."

"Thank you, Mr. President. I don't suppose there is any money connected with this award, is there?"

"I'm terribly sorry, David, but there is not. This way, it has no danger of becoming commercialized, demeaned or competed for in non-literary ways. Or so we hope."

"Well, I appreciate that, I suppose." He sighs. "But you know, most poets need money too."

"Yes, but it is my contention that while a poet should be paid for his work, he should not be paid for his prizes and awards. Those should be separate from money. They should be idealistic and spiritually real."

"I don't know, Mr. President. I just don't know if that is possible in this world. Anyway, thank you for The Galinsoga Award. It will probably make my daughter proud of me."

"Goodnight, Mr. Ignatow. And again, thank you for your faithful service all these years dedicated to the muse."

Bukowski was leering almost as much as the Devil had earlier. He said, "Well, well, well, poets are showing themselves to be a mercenary bunch, aren't they? Let's see, who's going to be the next poet to ask abut the cash? Okay, our next prize is The Viola Blanda Award or The 'Sweet White Violet' Award. Pres., you would get something like that in here. Or was that Diane's idea? 'Sweet White Violet'? Between you two, I wonder what I'm dong here. Shit you might as well give that 'Sweet White Violet' Award to my ex-wife's boyfriend, Manfred Anderson. Well, here it is. The award is given to two poets whose beautiful poetic voices are capable of seducng the most hardened listeners (hah, I'd like to see them get anywhere at all at the track. What a lot of malarkey.) These poets are the singers, the bards. Grace and lyricism are the strengths of their work. And tonight's Viola Blanda Award will be given to two poets, Galway Kinnell and W.S. Merwin. Are the gentlemen in the audience?"

I knew they weren't, but looked around to see if some new trick was going to be pulled out. No one stood up. I looked over to the gate wondering if they'd arrive magically as Ginsberg and Dorn had. But there was no one there. I looked back to the stage, just in time to see two small birds flying over to George Washington and settling on his arm. George held out his arm and said, "Merwin and Kinnell have sent their representatives to accept The Viola Blanda Award. They are both in Hawaii right now. Congratulations, little singers. We need the beauty of your voices in American poetry." The birds fluttered up over his arm and around his head for a minute and then flew off over the wall.

Bukowski turned to George and said, "This is a goddamn zoo, not a literary ceremony. I've gotta have another beer. Let's try some of that German stuff. I am getting tired of Red, White and Blue. Let's see. Next award. The Solidago Gigantea or The 'Goldenrod' Award which is to be presented to a poet whose voice is common, whose career in writing has been prolific, and whose poetry seems particularly native to the land and language of the United States. Ladies and Gentlemen, this evening we present The Solidago Award to two elder statesmen of American poetry, William Stafford and William Everson. Will you give the two Bills a hand? Step up here, Willy Stafford and Willy Everson."

Again, I looked around. Were they here? And sure enough, sitting very near the back, obscured by the shadow of a palm, were William Stafford and William Everson. Everson, formerly Brother Antoninus, was wearing a fringed buckskin jacket and a stetson hat. His long white hair hung down making him look like a cross between Buffalo Bill and Walt Whitman. He had a strong beaky profile in a face which looked both mild and ferocious, if that is possible. Stafford, his ruddy face glowing, was dressed casually as a retired English professor or insurance man might be. Both men were smiling at each other, and they walked slowly up to the stage. Stafford had a camera slung around his neck and when he reached the stage, he turned around, put the camera to his eye, and flashed a picture of the audience. Then, he turned to Everson and photographed him, and finally, he turned to where Bukowski was standing by George Washington and photographed the two of them together. I made a mental note to ask for a copy of *that* photo.

Bukowski turned to them. "Welcome, welcome. Have a beer. Good to see you old guys could make it. Are you going to ask about the money?"

Everson said, "I took a vow of poverty for years. It fit in very well with the life of the poet. I didn't really leave my order for money, but for love, for sex, for a rebirth in a world I had once not been able to understand."

"Just kidding. Just kidding," Bukowski waved his beer bottle. "Congratulations you two. William Everson. William Stafford. You are the first winners of The Solidago Gigantea Award in poetry."

Together Stafford and Everson said, "We are honored. Thank you."

They walk off stage and back to their table, dignified, both epitomizing so much that is extraordinary in the New American Poetry. I wished they were here to give readings, but knew that it was late and that this was not the occasion.

Bukowski looks tired and says, "I hate to admit this, but neither one of them is even 10 years older than me. I guess we're typically American in the poetry world too. Our old-timers aren't even over 70. I hate the thought that the world belongs to the young. Still I'm a young fellow, now that I hooked up with the health food chick."

I wondered what Bukowski really thought about age and aging. I never had thought that the process of growing old would be anything but natural in my life, as I had always thought of myself as a person who lived beyond the body, tried to accept it but at the same time to transcend it. But of course I had been deceiving myself. Being naturally healthy, even my bad habits had not required compensation when I was young. I had always had perfect skin. Pretty hair. A normal figure. But in my forties all that had changed. Only a constant concern for what I ate, what I drank, an attendance to vitamins, kept me going and didn't prevent hundreds of different allergic reactions, as well as chronic fatigue, the drying up of my skin into wrinkles and rashes.

To be truthful, I had always thought that I would be like Wanda

Landowska or Marianne Moore, one of those women who more or less looked the same when they were young and old. Slender and graceful. Blond turning to grey but not essentially looking any different. But this had not happened to me. And worse, I realized that I had travelled in and catered to a world which was youth-oriented and now was myself a derelict in that world. I wondered how Bukowski really felt about these things.

"This award, The Campion Award, otherwise known as The 'Sticking Cockle' Award or The 'Night Flowering Catchfly' Award will be given for a body of work by a poet which is difficult, sticky, so to speak, hard to penetrate (mmmmmm, just let me try) but which is original. And who else should receive this award than a poet I am sure you all know and hate (oops, sorry, just kidding), Clayton Eshleman. Give him a raspberry, folks. That's what he deserves. This guy had been bad-mouthing my poetry for years. I hope he's here tonight. I want to give him this award personally."

George Washington stood up. "Excuse me, Buk, but you know this award is a distinction. Actually, your own poetry was considered seriously in this category. But since we gave you The Orchid Award, we felt it unnecessary to also give you The 'Sticking Cockle' Award, though you probably would have relished the title far more."

"Give me another beer, Pres., this is getting ridiculous. Is Eshleman here?"

Again, I looked around but didn't see a sign of him. I was sure that if Clayton had been in the audience for the masque he would have spoken to me. Still, it is true that I really wasn't very much in the mood for talking to people. Knowing Clayton's involvement with the paleolithic caves, I wondered if some stagey device using that concept would be involved with his receipt of the award tonight.

Bukowski was talking again. "I'd never expect that Eshleman to be a no-show at anything honoring him. Eshleman, where are you?"

Coming in through the gate—I was watching, interested in what new gimmick might be used for this arrival—was Mother, the big rattler who had continued to frighten me whenever I saw her since my arrival late this afternoon. Naturally, in her mouth was a note. What other stage device was left? She was as big as the trunk of an old maple and probably eight feet long. There were no tables or chairs in the pathway from the gate to the stage. If there had been, they would have been cleared earlier by Dorn's horse and Ginsberg's float. But actually, this area was vast and seemed to me to get even larger, as if the space were expanding and the tables and chairs subtly moving farther and farther apart as the evening progressed. By now, I didn't even worry about whether it was another tromp d'oeil or simply part of the atmosphere of this place. Or my bad eyesight. It had begun to seem normal. The big snake arrived at Bukowski's feet. He didn't seem to show any fear, but actually Mother was heading for our President, G.W., and when she got to his table, she coiled up, slightly hissing and offered him the note held in her mouth. He took it, as if she were a dog and patted her head, in the same fashion. I could never imagine myself doing the same. It gave me a chilly sensation just to think about it. I didn't feel nearly as brave or foolish as I had when I simply told Mother to scat while we were alone in the conservatory.

George Washington stood up and said, "I have received the note from the winner of tonight's Campion Award, Clayton Eshleman. It says:

> The rotted man, inside animal, is a cactus weathered marrowless but still upright, even though the root connection dried up seasons ago.
> . . .
> The rotted man inside who used to seem archetypal, is biological . . . He is the new wilderness announcement that there is no longer a wilderness which has not been mixed with non-wilderness.
> . . .

He took the word 'order' and let it go"

Bukowski was leering again. "Well, Pres., there's certainly no doubt who wrote that, is there? I suppose that's code for 'I accept the "Sticking Cockle" Award.' Congratulations, Eshleman, you deserve it. Mother, scat. We don't need you on stage any more."

The snake hissed a little, uncoiled and slid away.

"Ninth award. We're getting through them. This is another category I am sure Diane must have thought up. The Gypsophila or 'Baby's Breath' Award and it will go to a poet or poets whose voices are delicate, quiet, innocent and new. 'Baby's Breath,' 'Sticking Cockle,' 'Sweet White Violet,' no wonder people hate poetry. Why aren't they giving the Budweiser Award, or the Olympia. The Olympia Award should be something for a poet to win, and it would have a little balls. Shit, give me another beer and let's get on with it. There are two poets receiving The Gypsophila Award. They are Robert Creeley and Michael McClure, both poets whose voices are delicate, while pervasive, fragile and new, often not perceived by the world as having much power. Robert Creeley and Michael McClure, are you guys here this evening?" He peers out into the audience, which now really seems like quite a large space to me.

Once again, George Washington stands up. "Buk, the gentlemen have sent telegrams. One says:

>   As I was walking
>   I came upon
>   chance walking
>   the same road upon.
>
>   As I sat down
>   by chance to move
>   later
>   if and as I might,

>   light the wood was
>   light and green,
>   and what I saw
>   before I had not seen
>
>   It was a lady
>   accompanied
>   by goat men
>   leading her.
>
>   Her hair held earth.
>   Her eyes were dark.
>   A double flute
>   made her move.
>
>   'O love,
>   where are you
>   leading
>   me now?'

and the other telegram said," George continued,

"GRRRRRRRRRRRRRRRRRRRRRRRRRRRRR. Thank you.' "

Bukowski turning to George, who was sitting down and beckoning the white gloved hands to pour him a cup of tea, said, "Some guys have style. Give me style anytime. Alright. The Cerastium or 'Chickweed' Award will be presented to new poets whose work seems special and distinguished, carrying on an observable tradition, but seeming to give it new possibilities. Tonight's Cerastium Award will be shared by Karen Snow, author of *Wonders,* and Frank Bidart, author of remarkable long poems such as 'Ellen West.' I know they are not here tonight. Ms. Snow wants to preserve her pen name anonymity, and Mr. Bidart is at the opera. Congratulations, Chicks. Welcome to The Society for Western Flowers.

"We've got two more awards coming up. The Lippia Lanceolata or 'Fogfruit' Award and The Nymphoides Peltana or 'Yellow Floating Heart' Award. The Lippia Lanceolata Award goes to a poet whose voice is deep and resonant of the past, though full of warning for the future. Tonight's recipient, and I know he is not here either, is Kenneth Rexroth. His poetry has contributed to the revolution in American poetry starting with Whitman and continuing into this century. Thank God, Rexroth isn't here tonight because he'd probably get up here and talk all night. Congratulations, Old Man, we all owe you a lot.

"The Nymphoides Peltana Award is for a poet who carries on an old tradition in new and subtle ways, and I cannot think of a better recipient of this award than Denise Levertov, whose poetry comes out of England's nineteenth century, carrying that lyrical and Romantic voice (you can tell, Diane wrote this stuff. Nobody in the world talks like this.) carrying the lyrical and Romantic voice over into a new prosody, the 'projective verse' which looks for its shape in the organic voice and life of the poet. Congratulations, Ms. Levertov, a new American poet honored tonight.

"Give me another beer. For Christ's sake, I'm glad that's over. I mean I like scribblers as well as anybody, but this shit seems to be right out of George Washington's camp cup tonight." He sits down, wringing wet with sweat.

"Thank you, Buk, for a fine job of mastering the ceremonies, and congratulations again for your own appointment to the Orchid rank of The Society for Western Flowers." George Washington is again standing at his table. "Let the party continue now. At dawn you will all be transported home, as you were brought here. In comfort and with pleasure, I trust. Once again, the new music group, The Moon's Shoes, will be playing for you under the direction of Ludwig V. Lunar, who seems to be back in his body." In actuality, it was the 2nd Beethoven, for Ludwig V. was still out-of-body.

George sat down and beckoned me to his table. I went up on stage and sat down with him. I was very tired, but didn't really feel that things were over yet for me. After all, whatever little epiphanies I had while wandering in the conservatory, I didn't really feel as if this evening had changed my life. It seemed to be summarizing my past and much that I thought and felt about the world; but as for giving me new directions, well, I didn't think that had happened. Still, I was very tired and I didn't really know what I would wake up tomorrow thinking.

"Diane, you still have work ahead of you, I think," said George.

"Yes, I know. But frankly, I was just thinking about how tired I am and how little an idea I have of what I could possibly do to understand my destiny better."

"Perhaps no one can be permitted to understand his destiny. You are only allowed to name your quest," he said.

"But I thought you meant for tonight to bring me some sort of realization." I felt confused.

"Diane, you are the inventor of tonight. I am only one of the actors in this drama."

"But I didn't invent you. I borrowed you from history. You already existed."

"Not in hot countries. You invented me into the desert and took me away from the East. You put me in the West. You have wanted to write my history as a new history."

He was right. But I simply was tired. "How can tonight change my life?"

"I doubt if it can," he smiled kindly at me. "No night does that. It is only what you think about tonight which can change anything, including yourself."

He was baiting and enticing me, and I knew I should stop talking, but somehow it just didn't seem possible. "What if I do not want to change?"

But he was still pretending to be reconciling, even though he was urging me on. "Surely there are many kinds of change. Some willed. Some inevitable. Perhaps you are changing all the time, though you have no desire to do so, and certainly do not will it. What then, Diane?"

"That's what I've always railed against. That's what I think is unfair. Why can't I at least have control over my own life?"

But he would not simply agree. "Diane, you can't *still* be asking that question at this point in your life? Have you not yet accepted the world as it is?"

I felt even more tired and now dejected. "No, it is rhetorical. I know how little control one has at best. But that little can be everything. I still believe that."

"Tell me, Diane, what have you learned from these years of questing? What have you found?"

"I don't think I have found anything. I have an aging body and an aging mind. But I didn't find them. They began to occur along the way. They are inevitable. And probably I have found nothing new."

"Then, if that is the case, aren't you ready for something else?"

"Maybe I am tired of questing. Maybe all I want to do is stop. Maybe I want to rest, not to find something new."

"Then you have indeed lost, haven't you? You must not have ever renewed yourself along the way."

I spoke now with only fatigue in my voice. "Questing is like war. It kills people, wears them out. Maybe questing is war."

"Are you really too tired to fight any more?"

"Most of the time. I don't think I'd even want to fight for Love, Sex, and Romance any more, either."

"What would you be willing to fight for?"

"I suppose I'd still fight for my ideas about poetry. I would be different though. I can't be incensed at stupidity and false notions, critics trying to write a false history of poetry or giving awards to the mediocre. I can be irritated, annoyed, sometimes even amused and go ahead, trying to teach my point of view, trying to give an alternate truth. I can't even be angry when I read Frederick Turner's 'A Polemic On Contemporary Poetry' which is a reflection of despair that comes from reading the least interesting poetry being written today (*Kenyon Review* stuff) and then feeling that poetry is dead. I almost don't even feel required to answer such a wrong-headed opinion about poetry, yet I suppose I will. But not with fireworks, which I certainly would have done in the past.

"The poets we gave awards to this evening are alive and well, in print, and if not winning Pulitzer Prizes, more importantly being read by serious readers across the country. I think in small ways I can help to extend this. The only person I don't seem to be able to help is myself. So few, so very few even seem willing to acknowledge what my poems attempt."

But George was continuing to play devil's advocate. "Perhaps you do not deserve that acknowledgement. Perhaps you have to earn it."

This made me angry. Even though I was tired, I exploded, "What do you mean, earn it? What have I been doing for the past twenty years?"

"Ah, you see there is a little fight left in you."

It seemed silly and pretentious and narcissistic to yell at George who was only trying to help me. "The anger is only momentary, I'm afraid. I apologize for exploding. It was silly. It came out of ego, not strength and knowledge."

"Ah, Diane, you will learn, you will learn. A new country is not easily formed. Even after it is fought for, you must keep renewing the ideas you fought for. They easily fade, and the habits of old conservatism relapse over them. One must have the mind of the seasons, constantly living with the cycle and expecting the death and rebirth that can come naturally, if you will permit it."

"Mr. President, you forget that we have four seasons, a cycle of climates only in the temperate zones, a small portion of the earth. In other portions of this planet's surface, the idea of season is ephemeral, and in other places static. Surely that has to be ackowledged in a vision of reality?"

"Diane, you know I cannot give you answers to such questions."

"Why not," I was exploding again as he seemed to deliberately be refusing to listen to reason. "Mr. President, you are not going to be guilty of that great American chauvinism of thinking the universe is like one small country, one place, one set of people? Us?"

"It is you, Diane, who extended my metaphor."

Now I was furious, though I didn't know what to do. Stamping a foot seemed silly. "No, it is not. You made your metaphor as if it were a universal. I question that!"

"Well, I am glad to see a little passion, Diane. Even if it is directed against me. Children have to rebel against their parents in order to claim their own lives."

"You smug man! I am not rebelling against you. Just trying to make you listen to reason."

George came as close to smiling as I ever saw him then. "Well, some might say that's all rebellion ever is."

His smugness really was infuriating me. "I can't stand your smugness, you old coot. You're as bad as the academic snobs who refuse to recognize Bukowski as a great poet."

"Well, Diane, I think it is time for you to sleep now. Rest. Prepare for your journey back to civilization, if one can call it that. I have enjoyed this evening very much and been extremely pleased to entertain you here at The Society for Western Flowers in the desert. I hope you will return in five years, when we will present another masque and another ceremony of awards. But perhaps you will be too far away on your new quest to join us."

Suddenly feeling sad, rejected and knowing again that I had failed, saying all the wrong things, sounding foolish and ignorant, I said, "I cannot imagine not coming here from anywhere I may be, even from death. And I still don't know what my new journey is, or if I have one, though you imply that it is already given to me. I know I am not The Moon any longer. Maybe I never was. No. I know that I once was. But tonight has made me see how far away I am from that nightly walk through the sky. Thank you, Mr. President. I love you."

"Be kind to yourself, Diane. Remember, even when you rebel, whose daughter you are. The King of Spain and I will always be watching over you. I wish you new countries, with many seasons. One foot in front of the other. One foot in front of the other. Good night, Daughter Moon."

His voice was hypnotic, and I was overcome with sleep. I remembered that those words, "one foot in front of another" were what he first said to me when I had been paralyzed with fear of the rattlesnake lying on the Cloudbound Kazak. I lay down on that now immense carpet, wrapped my black cloak around myself tightly, and fell asleep.

At dawn, I felt a tap on my shoulder, and there was the dalmatian, wearing his Tony Lamas boots. Lying beside me was a bird-of-paradise, the chiming flower from George's table, with which he had called the meeting to order, and I knew it was mine now. I also knew that the dalmatian was ready to drive me back to my real life, and though I was not myself ready, I knew that I had to re-enter the world where I would always be a little askew, where mind and body could never quite come together. We walked back through the labyrinth of glass, past the conservatory, and then the outdoor gardens, and finally out into the sage and scrub of the desert. I got into the back seat of the Oldsmobile, leaned back and thought, painfully, of my failures. With George. With my father. The evening of awards and allegory. The Wild Bergamot in the vase in the backseat of the car was drooping and I wondered if some water would revive it. Mercilessly, I threw it out the window and replaced it with George's chiming bird-of-paradise. Then I lapsed into the unforgiving thought of my life and its failures. It wasn't until an hour or so later that I came out of this tangled reverie and realized that we were travelling West instead of East, away from where I lived and towards California. Before I could say anything, I looked at the dalmatian who was slowing the car down and pulling over to the side of the road.

"What's the matter," I said.

"Nothing," he replied. And I realized it was the first time I had ever heard him speak. He braked to a final stop, turned off the ignition, removed the keys and tossed them back to me. Then he got out of the car, opened the back door for me, and as I looked wonderingly at him, he simply said, "It is your journey." I stood by the car. We were in open desert with purple and brown hill-mountains to the West. The highway was a black tongue, silent and empty. The dalmatian took off his Tony Lamas boots, his trousers and jacket, and laid them neatly down by the side of the road. On all fours, he leaped off the road and began running into the barren landscape. I didn't try to call him back. He had always seemed to know exactly what to do, but I did collect his costume and put it in the trunk of the car.

When I opened the lid of the trunk, I almost fainted. God, these Oldsmobiles have big trunks. There was Mother coiled up, and

hissing at me. But she immediately put her head into her coil and
went to sleep. She was only aroused by the opening of the trunk,
not by me. Beside her I saw my pansy mask and what looked like
a heap of diamonds, hundreds of marble- and walnut-sized glittering chunks. I was sure they were fake, but I liked the idea of
their being there anyway. There was also a stack of letters, all addressed to Diane Wakoski, The Desert, U.S.A. Or at least all of
them I looked at. I closed the lid of the trunk and walked around
to the side of the car. I got into the front seat, adjusted it for my
short legs, looked in the glove compartment for a map but found
no maps. I didn't know where I was anyway, so a map wouldn't
really help.

And I simply drove. Straight ahead. I was sure the car was
pointed West. Its tank was full of gas, and soon I would come to
some small civilization which would give me my bearings. For
this moment, I decided not to think of anything, but to concentrate on the movement of the car through this desert landscape; its
beauty had always seemed to belong to my life.

I realized that this moment was not genuinely different from any
other moment in my life. Once again I was not making a choice,
but simply following a road in which I had been left. I thought I
was travelling West, from the angle of the sun, but was not sure
of more than that. Still, I was moving through a desert, toward
an ocean. I did not really believe that anything was different.
What I carried with me even, I had not chosen. Snakes,
diamonds, letters, the mask of flowers, the world I inherited from
Lawrence and a few of his cronies.

* * *

There is a music slings itself toward me.
The voice of the desert,
dry and clear,
and my own flute which pipes me towards
the land shaped like an ear of corn.

Golden State, California.
I come from the pomegranate land;
I want to see the Golden Eagle find a voice,
one that sings a loud slot machine,
movie camera, six-lane freeway,
bikini and baby oil
sound,
one that allows the palm tree dry rattle
and harsh click of cactus needle
to blend with Mourning Doves and Linnets.
A Western voice.
There is a music slings itself toward me,
the sibilance of young men in old bodies,
the grunt of women broken open like figs, peaches, persimmons,
the bird-of-paradise, a spiky common flower
on our skin in this corn-eared land;
there is a music
and for that I search. One ear to the East, one ear
to the West, can there be a harmony?
There is a music slings itself toward me,
a long-haired woman sliding out of the ground,
her hiss,
out of the earth, Pythoness,
oracle, the lava spewing from the heaving mountain,
the music, scalding everyone who listens,
a music which announces
and outlives
death,
steaming, the hot breath,
renewing.

April, 1981

LOOKING FOR BEETHOVEN IN LAS VEGAS

The music in my head again,
not lily pad orchestra
or ebony flute,
the opening of yucca bells,
a creamy swish of lips,
the waver of pink and yellow,
Opuntia, cresting flesh,
Ocotilla flame, piercing air,
clear sound of the flowers.

My car pointed West,
the trunk full of diamonds,
and Mother rattler coiled there.
We are travelling to Southern California
to the Pacific,
where surfers
and angel-boy-men worship sun,
where the Osprey Sisters search for their piano,
where the moon bathes,
and the foggy canyons wrap their shot silk
around old bodies.

Still, there is a destination
which must be accomplished first,
a search for Beethoven in the
casinos of Las Vegas. Why
search for him
in this gaudy city
where ham and eggs are served
24 hours a day?
where dawn is dewy
but freshness is only in the mind,
the carpets permeated with smoke,
the uphostery stale with gin and perfume.
But I heard his sounds here once.

Never, in the subways of my city,
New York;
never, in the pounding of the Atlantic on steeply sloping beaches
when the sun nudged my tips
and wound round the sprocket of desire;
never, in the adobe missions
and terra-cotta roofs
of empty California life;
never, in the thick wheat-filled, asparagus-tipped, peach-laden,
  corn-spiked
summers or
ice-clotted winters
of Michigan;
not even on the cobblestone streets of Hydra, waking, caught like
  a cormorant,
with the ring around my throat, and looking
deep into the squid-clear Mediterranean;
or in the green-grey olive trees on the rocky hills of Majorca
where a man in pain was moaning in his cold kitchen.

I listened for his music
as I walked through Beethoven's park
in the Grinzingestrasse
Vienna spring, where I did hear
La Traviata and fancied as I wandered through the Schoenbrunn,
hearing Mozart's piano music accompanying my steps,
but I did not hear Beethoven's music
even elusively,
not once,
till I walked into the MGM Grand Hotel
and heard the thunk thunk thunk
of silver dollars
rattling into the slot machine tubs;
there it was,
thunk, thunk, thunk,
Beethoven's Sixth Symphony;
there it was,
a string quartet;

there it was,
the Appassionata Sonata;
Fidelio;
a Bagatelle;
thunk, thunk, thunk, thunk, thunk, symphonies
in George's coin,
the silver dollar from which
he had his Camp Cup made;
thunk, thunk, thunk,
this history of America,
that is,
the U.S.A.
played in a new symphonic thrust
when those silver dollars
clatter out of the machines in Las Vegas,
in the American desert,
the sound beyond The Strum,
the sound created by Beethoven, Americanized and
wandering in the desert,
looking for someone to love.

So, my journey has taken me there,
aching elbows, old acorns of the East
rattling in my empty joints,
making another music,
the one of aging and bone-crack death,
of sleeping alone and
tending the garden,
of looking out through the lacy curtains of one's life,
seeing the desert as the only future,
no strawberries on the lips now,
or moist canteloupe.

I hold in my hand a cardboard cup
as big as a child's head.
It is filled with silver dollars
I have received in exchange
for paper money. They weigh

down my hand
as the past has never weighed me down.
It is the future
which now is so heavy,
as heavy as a 6,000 B.T.U. air conditioner
or a small refrigerator,
or 24" pot with soil, containing a mountain ash tree.
As heavy as a mortgage and a house
your lover
doesn't want to live in.
It is the prospect of sleeping alone
every night, and the books
no one
will ever read.

It is the pain of your husband
swallowing sleeping pills in an anguish you can do nothing about,
or worse, your lover turning away from you
to other lovers,
or saying to you he would leave
you,
rather than hurt you/ you've
been hurt so much, but you
wondering why he doesn't think
leaving you
would be a source of pain.

When I dream of this city,
Las Vegas, I am
bare-armed,
long-haired,
scented with lilies of the valley
wrapped in raw silk,
shod in glass or gold,
looking nothing like
I ever looked in youth or life,
playing Chemin de Fer,
escorted by a man who wins at the dice tables, and I hear

Beethoven's symphonies
because they are big and melodic and my
life is big and melodic.

But when I am in this mythic city,
I am a small plump woman,
swathed in tent-like clothes,
sitting in the Keno parlour, reading
Henry James and playing 90¢ games.
I listen to the
thundering next to me in the bank
of slot machines, the tinkle,
the ringing,
and the thunk, thunk, thunk, thunk, thunk
of silver dollars
clanking into the metal pans.
It is Beethoven's music
but he is not here.
None of the men I love
are ever where
I look for them.
My map,
the Moon's map:
The Mare of Isolation,
The Mare of Remote Shadows,
The Mare of Longing.
No geography which would ever yield
what I have
searched for.

Driving West,
old, enlightened,
I still cannot fold up those
maps of lost goldmines,
abandoned trunksfull of diamonds,
of new countries and other planets.
I still listen for Beethoven at the ocean,
and George Washington in the desert.

But my own voice fades
into the landscape,
perhaps is only heard through
the unspoken language of desert flowers.

GREED, Part 13

The Greed For Control Over Death & Life

*In Homage To Beethoven, Bukowski, & Robert Turney,
Who Want All Of Life To Be Ecstatic*

7 February 1982

Today, brilliant sunshine on the deep snow, and my desire to listen to piano music and withdraw into myself. I feel angry with time, its effects on my body, my life, and yet in love with all those elements, like food and drink, which work the actual villainy. For weeks now I have been contemplating a *GREED: Part 13,* perhaps to be finished in time for publication with the COLLECTED GREEDs and to include "Looking For Beethoven In Las Vegas" as the bridge between GREED 12 and 13. I know I must try to begin tonight and have found this tempting springboard for myself, and I would like to quote an imaginary letter from Beethoven, written by James Goodfriend, the Masterworks Literary Editor for Columbia Records, to Fraulein von Kissow in Vienna, September 28, 1798, explaining his Opus 10 sonatas. I think I would like to use this as a paradigm for GREED 13 and will begin tonight if I can. I omit the beginning of the letter which is obviously written for verisimilitude.

* * *

"Streicher will have already taught you what a sonata movement is: two contrasting themes, or groups of themes, are expounded, the first in the *home* key, the second usually in its dominant, and the whole is then brought to a momentary close. The themes are then developed, and then restated, with the second group, this time also in the *home key,* and the movement is rounded off with a coda. This is a good outline, but there are many kinds of sonatas, and although they will all resemble such an outline, they may differ from it in a multitude of ways. See the first of the sonatas I have sent to you. It is in the key of C minor, and the second group of themes begins not in the dominant key, but in E-Flat major. This is not new at all, and I hope you will forgive me for belittling your learning should you understand it already. But see, the development section begins in C major. It begins with a bump, and they will put it down to my peasant manners. They do not understand such things. They know only pearly runs and arpeggios, pretty but meaningless. They cannot tolerate impolite violence.

But now I should show you that second movement (*Adagio molto*), too, is a sonata, and so is the third, but with this difference: that the slow movement has no separate development section at all, and that that of the third is only eleven measures long. And yet one does not mind the absence. First, because the one is so slow and the other so fast, and second, because the themes themselves are intricate enough, together with some slight variation, to keep one's interest from flagging. The finale is marked *prestissimo,* as you can see, but it must always be clear and even. This is a very impatient sonata, if you will, but it is one that has not been written before. You will know how to treat it.

There are many things in the F Major Sonata too, that will cause our general run of musicians to complain that things are not being done as rules specify, while some others will merely listen impatiently and not notice that there is anything unusual at all. You see the themes in the exposition — they are easy both to see and hear — but where are they in the development? They are not there. The whole development section is built on the little figure toward the end of the exposition, and, when the restatement arrives, it is in the wrong key. Such goings on! Only after the first theme has been restated in D does it come back to the home key, and then only the latter half does it. And yet, it is good so. The second movement, though it is marked *Allegretto,* is almost a slow movement in feeling; a real *Adagio* would be too heavy here, too stern, and would call too much attention to itself. The finale is a trick. It is a canon, of course. The first voice enters, and then the second at the octave, and then the third on the dominant. Ah, but look again. Suddenly it is no longer a canon, and a second little theme appears. Perhaps it is a rondo. But look still again. It goes into minor and begins to develop, and even before the development is through, the theme comes in in canon again, and after a lot of fuss, there is the second theme in the home key. It was a sonata all the time, even though it didn't sound in the least like it. What a disappointment! I can see you laughing over it now.

The third of the sonatas is very different. I would rather not say too much about it, except that it, and particularly the *Largo e mesto,* comes from the depth of my soul. I have never written a movement like this before, nor has anyone else. You, I believe, will understand me, but I fear few others will, even those who can bring themselves to accept the strangeness of my other music. This movement is like a terrible tragic presentiment, and yet I feel strongly drawn to it. Play it for yourself. Tell me what it says to you."

* * *

Sonata No. 5 in C Minor,
Op. 10, No. 1

The Pot of Bouillebaisse

to Kurt & Gillian Heinzleman

Allegro molto e con brio

> (You know you are in an extraordinary
> American household when you come, as a
> stranger, and your hosts have planned to
> take you out to dinner, but the time slips
> away and suddenly there is no time before
> the evening program, and your hostess suggests
> it would be better simply to eat leftovers
> from the fridge, and what she produces is a
> fine pot of bouillebaisse. This, in Texas,
> is a certain finesse.)

What is natural,
nature,
that it holds such a false (unnatural)
place
in our estimation?

The broth has

a faint hint of saffron,
those stamens of the crocus, fine as eye-
lashes which are gathered meticulously
by girls with silk fingers,
and is tinted by sex of this spring flower
here in Southern Texas.
This is the city where I smelled flowering
cherry
one spring
that was like tortillas,
and it is the city which also houses
a Gutenberg Bible,
as well as a few stubs from
Hemingway's cigarette-smoking days.

Now I eat this
stew from Mediterranean waters.

Adagio molto

      She says she cannot be
photographed — but
what does a camera show?
Imogen Cunningham perfectly
presents the magnolia bud,
as woman, the center, a
breast thrust into warm Southern night,
lips as petals, articulation
of spike and cream of flesh.
Outerbridge
shows the egg balanced
unpierced on the sharp triangular tip
of a pyramid;
Herbert Lizt shows the leg & wiggling painted toes
in sand next to a dal-
matian;
the surfaces,
the places where beauty

can be focused.

I have married a camera
over and over again,
to try to capture the power of
those surfaces. How many
reflecting surfaces my young body
and face have had. How
much more photogenic I have been
than beautiful.
                    Bones,
you say,
but my bones were never special/ only
my desire to strip away flesh,
to reveal bone,
any bone, only my desire to
leave flesh,
never having had the flesh
of magnolia.

But you, Gillian, cuddling lover
of dachshunds,
violist who doesn't like any of the
conductors
in Texas,
Latin scholar,
medievalist,
in your red flannel gown and love
of old New England oak,
whose father ran the Morgan Library,
you, whose refrigerator held the
saffrony rich left-over bouillebaisse,
whose speech is witty and who is
completely, unselfconsciously
married to an
Adonis,
you poignantly show me
the fatuousness

of planing, honing, focusing,
reflecting surfaces. No matter
their beauty,
they never show what's embodied.

They,
surfaces,
they replace interiors
whenever any value is placed upon them. Of course you cannot
be photographed. Your little face
with its snaggle teeth
and constant frown of concentration,
your soft black hair which falls
like untidy leaves over your forehead,
your little round belly, which we all get, who
sit often hunched over our books,
your round round shoulders for the same reason,
and stumpy little gardening hands,
they must all show ridiculously
on film/ for you
have never believed civilization's
lie/ of surfaces;
somehow more truly than the rest of us
you believe Plato's suggestions
that we are expressions of our souls.

Around me daily are perfect
magnolias,
beautiful eggs,
model-quality legs.
Surely one or two possesses a soul;
some must even have beautiful
minds or spirtual decency.

More likely, though,
they *are* those surfaces,
for that is where the focusing
has been. Why did I love

the camera's eye?
Because I
could lie to it. And surely
somewhere there is
the photographer
who could be your lover,
who would see you naked and curved
as one of Botticelli's women,
black hair falling around a shell-
like face, as water is perfect
unordered grace.

The bouillebaisse came out of this
sea with you,
your feet small and white, sea anemones.
On your face, the intelligent frown
of musical concentration.
Perhaps in soft focus it will reveal
the counterpoint you love
where a perfect musical idea
is worked out horizontally,
where, when complete, it will yield the balance of the vertical
too.

How can we live in a world of cameras
and permit them
to do so
little?

Finale: prestissimo: World of The Natural

This exquisite bowl of soup,
the salt of a sun-shot sea,
filmy anemones brushing
the tongue. The flesh
beyond scale and bone,
white and firm, the hint of crocus-

flowered stamen,
flower soup,
from the sea.

This and other perfectly prepared,
deliciously ingredienjted eating,
has padded my bones,
made great blobs of fat on arms,
belly, turned my legs into hams,
my face back into dough.
It is age and slow metabolism,
rising blood pressure, swollen
ankles, like footballs,
the surfaces and planes of some-
one else,
my mother,
an old woman,
a ragbag body.

Why can't I believe
this is natural
rather than ugly? False definitions?
   —a lifetime of not wearing
     cosmetics, and a definition
     of beauty as stemming from
     the unadorned perfection of
     organic shapes?

What is a weed?
                A plant we
                don't cultivate?
                One,
                we would rather not
                have in the
                garden?
Is a rose
natural?
                Yes, but so is

                    that stuff which used
                    to take over our Southern California yards,
Johnson Grass.
So is milkweed,
and mullein.
The common dandelion,
And a tomato, or bell pepper,
            if you are in the right
            part of the world.

Weston's photos
of the undulating canyon walls
of green pepper,
the sweet, filled flesh of
this fruity vegetable
baring its surfaces/
                would he
have photographed the old wrinkled
thing they become?
when having lain in the market or vegetable bin
too long?
            But then, there is
springy little Imogen C.
who came into
her own
as an old lady, and who
photographed other
old people
to contrast with the thrilling flowers
of her young eye/ how
I wish I had Molière's tongue,
interpreted by Wilbur, or the
flower language of Levertov or Duncan, even
the salty speech of Olson,
Oh, Gillian, how I wish I had your
wisdom of interiors,
when the camera tongue
lashes me
now.

* * *

Sonata No. 6 in F Major,
Op. 10, No. 2

for Robert Duncan

Allegro

The movement is toward the sea.
Or the land
which is by a sea,
magenta bougainvillea (whispering) with its
papery lips a language
of terra-cotta roofs,
flagstone terrace,
calla lily white-washed adobe,
a promontory of dry cliffland
with dry cypress clinging to its California face.
Am I going
to the edge of the sea
to await the sailor?
the one whose gold tooth flashes
when he deals the cards
or trims the sails?
Who is he,
if my father is dead,
and my lover home
in bed?

The movement is to water/ warm water,
to diving porpoises and seals,
to the extinct sea otter and the nearly
gone Galapagos turtle,
to the trigger fish, angels and clowns
of warm waters,
away from trout, steelhead, salmon, firm fleshed lovers of
cold stream, icy currents.

Allegretto: The Office Down The Hall From Me

The heat of September rises
from the ground like snow vapor
hovering around the peaks of
the Andes,
and I hurry down the polished
corridor to my office,
past the elevator I never use,
past an office with an open door
which was used last year by
people who had
stacks of untidy file folders sitting on their desks
and the floor,
who drank endless cups of coffee and smoked and never noticed,
I'm sure,
their surroundings.

Now, the open door stops me
with my own sweaty pile of papers
and bulging canvas bag of books.
The room has been transformed:
symmetrically placed in the center
of the room
is one desk sitting on a red and blue
Scandinavian rug,
the rug, like a tropical parrot
from a Brazilian jungle
shot down to this floor.
And on the walls to the left,
a hand woven cotton fabric with the stripes and arrows of a
certain mountain village.
Perfectly, in the corner,
near the window,
is a tall cheese-leaved
philodendron, and neatly around the walls
are tidy bookcases, full of seriously bound
books.

Who has transformed this dingy room?
I expect a woman with purple and yellow shawls,
or a man who might
look like Simon Bolivar
(whom I studied in 6th grade),
But the room is empty and I walk
past it to my autumn office,
and once I've turned the key, forget this
traveller from Sweden & South America.

Once when I go to the bathroom,
back down the same hall,
that day, I pass a tall man
who looks rather like Abraham Lincoln.
He is talking to a fat man
and a woman whose ears stick out.

Another day
going to the restroom to get
jugs of water for the spider plant, palm and
fig in
my office, I see him again.
Not really Abraham Lincoln,
but a cartoon of him.
He stands awkwardly, but stiff, twig-like,
his beard, trimmed straight
juts out from a flat face
which looks pushed in, a bit
midget-like. He has
a little bulbous nose and
short arms. Heavy eyebrows
and a laser gaze. He looks a little like
one of the scruffy crew
who moved out of the iguana office,
but like an older brother,
tidier, more
definitive.

A few days later
I walk past the open door again.
This time, the cartoon Abe Lincoln
is standing like a statue
inside the office. The next
time I see him, he is nailing
a picture on the one still-empty
wall.

A cartoon has transformed
this dingy office,
has made an elegant
South American reception room.
Why should I find this so disturbing? Perhaps that he cannot
transform his cartoon face
and body into a real
Abe Lincoln look-alike.
If this is what he can do
to his office,
why not his person?

Still,
still, each time I pass him
in the halls, I think of
two eminent
American critics of contemporary poetry, one of whom
has sneered at my work,
the other slighted and ignored it,
two personages in the world of literature
whose power I have feared and envied,
seeing them for the first time,
a few months ago
(and being astonished)
to find that one
looks like Little Lulu's aunt,
or, more accurately, like Little King's wife,
the other both looks and sounds like

Woody Woodpecker.

Is there some poetic justice
which makes us all
into cartoons
when we misuse power
or take ourselves too seriously?

What am I doing taking
surfaces so seriously?
Little King's wife dismissed me
because of one quickly reflecting surface
she saw. How I resent
this,
and am glad to assign
an equally uncomplimentary surface
to her./ But where
is the world where surface
& interior
can harmonize?
Why the mind and body so recal-
citrantly
unwed?

Presto: Thank You For The Phalanopsis

for Eric

and the fresh lichee nuts which were
moldy and spoiled
when they arrived, generously,
enthusiastically packed into another pepper
tin, feaster, friend,
to whom I wish
I could give some of the gifts
longed-for
and deserved — you said you'd

like
a dozen plain white shirts,
so that you'd always have
a clean one
to wear to work,
and you also need, more than
the shirts,
one or two talented actors,
actresses; a company
who would perform your
                       strange
wonderful plays,
more challenging than Merce Cunningham's dances
or, even, Cage's music,
though related to both.
Why is it
so hard to give
real
art
to the world? Not
beauty,
but truth?
        Who told
that lie/
       that they belong
together, are
the same?

Only in youth, surely?
That poet must
have died young.
What about the rest of
the world,
those of us
who live to be the shrivelled
bell pepper with moldy spots,
or the sour, rotting
(once so sweet) lichee nuts

which came in the can to me
last year,
another unacceptable
work
of art?

* * *

Sonata No. 7 in D Major,
Op. 10, No. 3

The Drunk Sonata

*for Bukowski, Beethoven, & "Bobbie" T., the three
"B"s in my life*

Presto

Bad music
makes a bad life. I've
said this before,
not Olson's "musick, mu-sick" on the street car,
but worse, the loud rapacious
rhythms which prophesy false sexuality
and batter the senses
with longing for unearned fame, one
                             moment
and a thousand fans, seduction
leading
to the fall, fashion bombarded with
the punishing snake, oh poets,
rescue us from The Rock,
false instruments used for false music,
Leave Mick Jagger and the gang in their stoney
corridors. Release your ears
for a music which understands silence.

Largo e mesto

Heal thyself, Diane,
I beg, as you insist that by living with the sick
one becomes sick; yet I resist
the image
of nurse dying of patient's contagion/ while all too well
I know Father Damien finally contracted
leprosy,
the price of his human willingness to touch and relieve.

I want to heal someone I love,
but he bombards my strength with his diseases.
Will I get lung cancer from his four cigarette packs smoked daily?
and breathed into my lungs?
Will his drinking and the demons like bad genies which
come out of the rubbed bottles gleaming
through
his night finally destroy my equilibrium, my
ability to concentrate, my structures and life?
Will his inability to love
consistently, his self-hate and adolescent music
become my own feelings?
What do you do when you sleep alone every night
because he is sitting above you in a drab room,
staring at the walls,
fighting demons from bottles in a cloud of
he-man Marlboro smoke,
with the Rolling Stones blaring cryptic porn-ocracy?

Do you listen
to Beethoven or read 19th century
English novels about oppression from outside structures
and their authors' fantasies of escape? Do you
tend your plants and hope that they will themselves
collectively raise their leaves
against the demons,
the smoke,

the brooding razor blades slashes
in the arm,
the broken bones and bloody scrapes of alcoholic stumbling?

Every day I tell myself how lucky
I am
that he is still alive,
for despite these things, I love and need,
can only think of a final horror: his death,
my losing him/ and at
that point how lucky I would feel myself
if he were only stumbling blindly, yeastily
to bed, thrashing and moaning in his final 5 a.m.
sleep after the ghosts and devils
have beat him all night.
How can I tell him to forget
whatever it is that troubles him,
to take his life simply,
live it day by day, savouring the innocent joy
of still being able to breathe,
of not living in a war-ravaged time,
of not having to work at demeaning or killing jobs but
the gift of life
is not mine
to give,
and he
does not
claim it for himself.

Oh, Beethoven, you never forgot your art. How
lucky all of us are, who
can claim something we believe in,
who can give ourselves constantly
some sense of promise.

Menuetto: Allegro

Your eye, Robert,

such a fine eye, whether for mushrooms,
sago palms, or the cockatoo hair scallops of a South African
novelist, the smokey dreams
of a sad academic
curling around his head as burning latakia.
How clear it is in your photographs/ those demons
who cloud your vision at night
are sadistic Marlboro men, riding down to a
Western circle of hell, lassoing you, dragging
you with them; they come out of a bottle,
bad genies, obscure your vision;
yet that clear photographer's eye
could be
the ghost trap
to bring them down.
You have a vision.
Available light, that's what you specialize in/
sleep, sleep,
photographer, at night,
when the light is false.
Wake at dawn when the white curtains
move with a coolness
of pale tulips,
the moon still in the sky watching over
your sleep, so that you can rise
clear-eyed, each day,
and live in radiance,
not the darkness only a flash (false) light
can enter.

Rondo: Allegro

Gillian, share your vision with both of us,
poet and photographer,
beyond surface,
beyond the shadow detail,
into the body, the substance, the reality,
which obscures false light.

The magic pot of soup in your Texas refrigerator,
one spoon-full of this bouillebaisse
with the tongues of spring crocus seasoning it,
the white flesh of fish
Robert loves to catch,
one spoonful
and vision is given, clear vision,
and the photographer smashes the attic full
of bottles, a collective whimper goes up
into mid-Western air, as bad genies
are severed and crushed, their ghost-life ended
finally as the eye
shrinks them, shrivels them,
and Lord Duncan, Lord Moon, enters this place,
takes the demons with him in Dionysian ritual,
the poet restoring order,
the bony moon, earthy light, sucks the deadly
orgone energy out of Robert's aerie.

I conjure this.
I ask Gillian to conjure this.
I, magician, wish this.
I, lover of Robert, will this.
I, moon, Admirer of Lord Robber Baron Moon Poet, Duncan,
call for this,
I, student of Beethoven, invoke this.
Good music.
Good magic.
Words of Spring Ritual, renewal of life after
a sojourn in Hell,
eye of the photographer,
I sing to your vision.
The cool moon coming through
paper narcissus curtains,
shining on a still face, shaded all night
in sleep from the demons,
shaded from
false light.

Printed May 1984 in Santa Barbara and Ann Arbor for the
Black Sparrow Press by Graham Mackintosh & Edwards Brothers, Inc.
Design by Barbara Martin. This edition is published in paper
wrappers; there are 300 hardcover trade copies; 200 hardcover
copies have been numbered & signed by the author; & 50 numbered
copies with an original holograph poem have been handbound in
boards by Earle Gray & are signed by Diane Wakoski.

Photo: Robert Turney

DIANE WAKOSKI was born in Whittier, California in 1937 and educated at U.C., Berkeley. She has published thirteen collections of poems, and many other slim volumes. Her two most recent collections of poems from Black Sparrow were *Cap of Darkness* (1980) and *The Magician's Feastletters* (1982). The U. of Michigan Press published her criticism in *Toward a New Poetry* (1980). She is currently Writer in Residence at Michigan State University.